Artificial Intelligence a Modern Approach

Discover the Best Techniques for Beginners and the Revolutionary Advantages of Artificial Intelligence and Its Business Application to Achieve Better Results

Anderson Coen

Description

This book is written in clear and understandable language to help beginners in learning the concepts, techniques, and algorithms of artificial intelligence. In an effort to brief the implementation of AI in business and real life, the concepts are briefed with suitable examples so that readers can adapt the given information in the first read.

Artificial intelligence has revolutionized the work process and capabilities of computing systems. With the ability to learn and adapt to changes over time, artificial intelligence and machine learning models will continue to bring positive improvements in today's world. Most importantly, artificial intelligence is bringing amazing advantages in the education, finance, commerce, health care, and information technology industry. By learning the concepts and findings explained in this book, readers can develop a deep understanding of how artificial intelligence actually works and what are the main reasons for its continuous growth in industry and business.

The rules and techniques of artificial intelligence work under predefined algorithms and processes. To make readers understand the searching and training process in artificial intelligence models, each algorithm and search process is clearly explained along with diagrams and descriptions. Furthermore, the book covers all of the major and minor concepts, methodologies, and techniques of artificial intelligence to ensure convenient learning for the readers.

After reading this book, readers will definitely be able to analyze the performance and prediction capabilities of AI models. Artificial intelligence methods and theories are developed to bring long term facilities and advantages to humans in the future.

Table of Contents

Introduction

The study of artificial intelligence (AI) is based on how the human brain thinks, decides, and takes action for certain scenarios. In today's world, technology is increasing with each second which is bringing great revolution and facilities for people. To make computers work intelligently, we have to work in the findings and principles of artificial intelligence and deep learning. Artificial intelligence is a branch of computer science that is concerned with automating processes on the basis of human intelligence.

Techniques and methods of artificial intelligence are used to build machines that are capable of making decisions on their own. With the help of AI, we can develop software and information systems which are capable of performing specific tasks without being explicitly programed. With less human intervention, artificial intelligence systems can solve problems and generate outcomes as well. Major goals of AI and machine learning are to solve knowledge intensive tasks and replicate human intelligence as well.

Machine learning and artificial intelligence is widely used in mathematics, biology, computer science, statistics, sociology, and psychology disciplines. There are great advantages of artificial intelligence as AI machines deliver high accuracy and have the capability to make proper decisions as per the given training data. Moreover, AI systems provide high reliability and fast decision making which can bring long term benefits to businesses and change the way we are performing everyday tasks.

Chapter 1: What is Artificial Intelligence?

Artificial intelligence is defined as a branch of computer science through which we can develop intelligent machines to behave, think, and make decisions like humans. With artificial intelligence models, there is no need to program the computer systems repeatedly because they have the capability to learn and make predictions on their own.

History of Artificial Intelligence

The development of digital computers began in the 1940s and they were demonstrated to be programed for performing various tasks. In 1936, the Turing machine theory was defined by the British mathematician Alan Turing. The theory proved that the Turing machine or a computing machine would only be able to execute a cognitive process when divided into multiple steps that are represented through an algorithm. This is the main driving force behind artificial intelligence as most of the AI systems and machine learning models are based on the same approach. The world's first artificial intelligence program was written by a group of scientists in 1956 who believed that the aspects of learning of human intelligence could be replicated by machines.

Dartmouth Conference, which was organized by American computer scientist John McCarthy, was the event where artificial intelligence was first adopted. In the 1960s, data scientists and researchers began to focus on developing algorithms that are capable of solving geometrical theorems and mathematical problems. Working on artificial general intelligence, big data and deep learning has started from 2010 with the launch of high-performance AI systems and machine learning models.

The first AI winter concept is based on the unavailability of breakthroughs on which the British and U.S government decided not to research further on artificial intelligence. Because of this step, the enthusiasm and willingness of scientists to do research on AI and its practices began to decrease in 1974. Furthermore, AI researchers did not receive funds and relevant opportunities to work and develop further on the concepts of artificial intelligence.

Soon after the first event of AI winter, artificial intelligence was restarted in the form of "expert systems." These systems were also considered as the programs that answer specific questions and bring solutions to problems for a specific domain. Moreover, there are two main types of expert systems that are named, "knowledge engine" and "inference engine." Knowledge engine represents rules and facts for a specific topic whereas inference engine applies facts and rules from knowledge engine to derive new facts. This process was then continued by the second AI winter which was developed in the early 90's (Lasse, 2018).

Understanding AI

The concept of artificial intelligence is designed to give computers the ability to perform tasks on their own without being explicitly programed. This term is frequently used for the project development of systems that are based on characteristics of humans. These characteristics include the ability to understand, interpret, discover meaning, and make decisions which can yield the best outcomes. Whether it's to discover proofs of complex mathematical theorems or automated vehicles, artificial intelligence is continuously being developed and researched to bring better solutions for businesses and humans.

Defining Intelligence

Intelligence is described as the human behavior to perform specific tasks. Human intelligence is not a single trait but a combination of diverse abilities that are combined to finish a complex activity. This process covers perception, language interpretation, problem solving, reasoning, and learning which are also the basis of artificial intelligence. There are different forms of learning that are applied to artificial intelligence, such as learning through trial and error.

Generalization involves the application of past experience to analyze new situations and allows computer programs to make the best decisions on their own. To create inferences for a situation, scientists use a reasoning approach to classify between inductive or deductive information. In the inductive cases, the truth of premises is dependent on the truth of guarantees whereas for the deductive cases, the truth of premises is based on the truth of the conclusion.

The data collected to develop tentative models is meant to be true in each case so that the artificial intelligence models could deliver accurate results. Furthermore, deductive reasoning can also be used in artificial intelligence model development because it is based on the concepts of logic and mathematics.

Problem-Solving and Perception

The aim of artificial intelligence is to deliver accurate insights and predictions through machine learning models. Problem solving in AI is considered as a systematic search through a range of possible actions to finish the process. In artificial intelligence, a special purpose method is created to solve a particular problem and includes specific features to solve a problem, whereas through a general-purpose method, data scientists can solve a variety of problems by applying a single method.

In the perception approach, machine learning and artificial intelligence engineers perform in-depth analysis and evaluation before working on a solution. The environment is fully studied by means of real or artificial approaches to explore the hidden relationships in data. Furthermore, the intensity and direction of scenarios is also overviewed to design a suitable solution based on artificial intelligence theories. Machine learning and artificial intelligence models tend to develop strong problem-solving skills with experience. During the training procedure, if the model is given high quality data, it can yield amazing outcomes and bring positive results as well. Moreover, supervised learning AI models also have the capability to learn from datasets and improve its performance over time.

Reasoning

The process of drawing inferences to achieve a proper solution is known as reasoning. In other words, we can say that reasoning is the process to infer facts from known or existing data and it is generally linked to derive relevant solutions in artificial intelligence. Furthermore, reasoning is also mandatory to make machines able to think rationally and similar to human brains, allowing artificial intelligence models to behave like human beings. There are different types of reasoning which are explained as follows:

Deductive Reasoning

Deductive reasoning is the process of acquiring new information from logically and related-known information. This includes data with complete attributes and variables and is a valid form of reasoning in artificial intelligence. With deductive reasoning, the argument's conclusion should always be true whenever the premises are true. Furthermore, this is also a category of propositional logic in artificial intelligence and includes the implementation of different facts and rules. Furthermore, it is also known as top down reasoning because the truth of premises is dependent on the truth of the conclusion.

For example: All human beings eat vegetables and John is a human. We can also conclude that John eats vegetables.

Inductive Reasoning

The inductive reasoning process in artificial intelligence is a type of reasoning which is used to arrive at a conclusion through the process of generalization. By using limited sets of facts, it starts with the processing of specific data or facts and automatically reaches a conclusion. Furthermore, inductive reasoning is also known as bottom up reasoning or cause-effect reasoning because it provides support to the conclusion.

For example:

Premise: Each of the cats in the zoo are brown.

Conclusion: We can expect all the cats to be brown.

Abductive Reasoning

Abductive reasoning is a type of logical reasoning which begins with single or multiple observations. These observations are used to find the best suitable conclusion or explanation for the said observation. In abductive reasoning, we cannot use the premises to guarantee the conclusion because it is an extension of deductive reasoning. For example, we can say that the football ground is wet if it is raining as an implication whereas the axiom can be stated as the football ground is wet. As a conclusion we can say that it is raining. Abductive reasoning is a major portion of artificial intelligence model development and is used to derive multiple solutions for a specific problem.

Common Sense Reasoning

Common sense reasoning can be gained through experiences and is an informal type of reasoning. It is dependent upon a good judgement rather than heuristic knowledge and exact logic. For example:

1. One car can be parked at a time.
2. If you jump without a parachute, you can face severe damages to your body.

The statements written above show clear examples of common-sense reasoning that are easily understandable by human beings.

The Need for AI

Artificial intelligence is a technique to simulate the workings of the human brain so that machine and computer systems can work without being explicitly programed. Nowadays, we are in need of AI systems and machine learning models to complete everyday tasks with ease. Although it is a good approach to automate tasks, on the other hand, it can yield several negativities for humans. The approach saves manpower an organization needs to complete a specific operation and increases the overall efficiency as well. Moreover, artificial intelligence helps businesses to achieve their targets and improve sales within a short period of time.

Majorly, artificial intelligence has the capability to make digital systems achieve higher levels of capabilities and increase their overall performance as well. Due to the increasing number of day to day tasks, data scientists have to develop machine learning models that have the capability to make accurate predictions and deliver long term benefits to businesses as well. Additionally, automation of processes in industries can be made possible through machine learning and artificial intelligence in order to achieve the best outcomes.

Types of Learning

The ability of technology to learn and act smarter is based on artificial intelligence models and machine learning systems. Artificial intelligence is promising because it changes the complete procedure of writing code to generate software programs. Instead of programming in the conventional way, we can actually tell the computer what to do and how to perform specific tasks. In artificial intelligence, there are three major forms of learning which are known as assisted learning, unassisted learning, and reinforcement learning.

In the assisted learning approach, the machines are fed with predefined inputs and outputs. The information is also used to generate high quality datasets and once the machine has started to learn from the training set, it can be considered as completely trained. Furthermore, machine learning and artificial intelligence models will only train properly if the training data is properly defined or has appropriate relationships between variables and attributes. For the unassisted learning approach, the machine is fed with predefined data but has to figure out the operations and relationships between datasets on its own.

Reinforcement learning is also known as goal-oriented learning because whenever a machine is given a proper goal to achieve, it can make relevant decisions based on the approaches learned from the training data. A common example of reinforcement learning are video games in which the machine is determined to win the game. In this way, the system will determine and find the best suitable ways to make the best decisions in each situation.

Goal of AI

Researchers and data scientists are continuously working on bringing day to day improvements in artificial intelligence systems. The technology is bringing new revolutions and improvements in business and industrial processes along with giving ease to humans as well. Furthermore, artificial intelligence is absolutely going to revolutionize how humanity thinks about the role of reality and culture. Most of the time, technology acts smarter than human beings and allows machines to make decisions that will bring long term benefits. Although there are some myths and misconceptions about the increasing involvement of AI in the real world, researchers and scientists are working continuously to make machine learning and deep learning models suitable for human beings in each case.

In early days, machine learning and artificial intelligence were used to develop problem solving reasoning skills through appropriate knowledge representation. Knowledge representation allows machines to interpret and understand information which in return helps in making accurate and productive decisions. The goal of AI is to develop intelligent machines that have the capability to learn on their own.

Furthermore, researchers can develop machines which have the power to read and understand human languages through natural language processing approaches.

Advantages

Intelligent machines are designed to deliver accurate data insights, predictions, and solutions. As they have the capability to perform complex tasks which cannot be done by humans, artificial intelligence machines provide increased efficiency and ease to humans in different ways. There are thousands of information systems and applications developed through artificial intelligence such as autonomous cars, voice recognition systems like Siri, and interactive robots.

With the help of AI technology, scientists are able to develop digital assistants which are great performers and yield better efficiency. Furthermore, the need for a human workforce has been greatly reduced in industries and corporate sectors due to the implementation of artificial intelligence systems and machine learning models. Artificial intelligence enables accuracy and speed levels which were impossible to achieve from traditional computing systems. Due to the massive growth in unstructured data, data scientists have to produce machine learning models that are capable of understanding and manipulating data without human intervention.

Furthermore, operational efficiencies and increased productivity are the main reasons behind the widespread use of artificial intelligence. Objectives of AI research include knowledge representation, natural language processing, ability to manipulate and move objects, learning, and planning. As there are long term goals defined for general intelligence sector, the technology is constantly being developed and improved.

Chapter 2: Basics of Artificial Intelligence

Emerging technologies are based on artificial intelligence, machine learning, and deep learning theories as they have resulted in bringing amazing innovations. In machine learning, data scientists take support from big data to train models accurately for which data needs to be collected from multiple resources. For understanding concepts of natural language processing, deep learning, data analytics, and data mining, we are required to get in-depth knowledge about the basics of artificial intelligence.

Understanding Machine Learning

Machine learning is a sub-branch of artificial intelligence and is based on the concepts and theories of AI. Similar to humans, the information systems developed with machine learning have the capability to retain information and develop strong predicting skills in the future. Generally, machine learning is a type of artificial intelligence that allows machines to make decisions on its own without any kind of human intervention. Furthermore, the models designed with machine learning and artificial intelligence theories can deliver accurate insights and conclusions that might be impossible to be done by humans.

Similar to a human brain, machines can get smarter and retain information for a longer period of time but they are not susceptible to things such as information overload, distractions, or short-term memory loss. In general, machine learning is also known as the process to complete artificial intelligence functions because it is dependent on the rules and outcomes of artificial intelligence.

In machine learning, an input layer is provided with a dataset through which intelligent machines learn and identify patterns in the dataset for making accurate decisions. Furthermore, it is mandatory to understand how machines learn from training data before we head towards the model development procedure.

Parts of Machine Learning

The key components of machine learning are known as representation, evaluation, and optimization. In the representation phase, data scientists work on how to present knowledge which includes concepts of decision trees, graphical models, support vector machines, and neural networks. Evaluation is done to overview the performance and accuracy of machine learning programs and is completed through various methods including squared error, posterior probability, prediction and recall, accuracy, and margin. Furthermore, optimization is a technique to generate programs which are also named as search processes.

Machine learning algorithms have the ability to retrieve information from external sources, fetch useful data, and start working any given scenario to make accurate predictions and data insights. To achieve the best results, it is advised that the artificial intelligence and machine learning models are trained on labeled and high-quality datasets only. In this way, the model will develop the ability of self-learning and provide accurate prediction results in the future. Remember that machine learning models are prone to error and if they are not properly trained, you might not be able to get the best results.

Types of Machine Learning

Machine learning is divided into three main subcategories which are supervised learning, unsupervised learning, and reinforcement learning. Generally, supervised and unsupervised learning methods are used regularly in machine learning model development whereas reinforcement learning is best suited for solving complex problems.

Supervised Learning

Supervised learning is the most used type of machine learning to develop AI models. Because it is based on simple approaches and theories, data scientists can create great performing AI and machine learning systems through supervised learning techniques. A labeled dataset is provided for supervised learning because a machine is supposed to learn from past experiences. Whenever the model is given training on a labeled dataset, the process is known as supervised learning. Furthermore, the given data has proper labels, variables, and attributes which make it easier for the models to get trained and make accurate predictions in the future. Once fully trained, the supervised learning algorithm will have the power to predict and observe new situations without any problems.

This approach is classified into two main categories which are classification and regression. A classification problem occurs when the output variable belongs to a specific category such as "blue" or "green" whereas the regression problem occurs when the output variable is defined as a real value such as "age" or "name."

Unsupervised Learning

Unsupervised learning is a category for training machine learning models in which the input data is completely unlabeled and unclassified. The machines are supposed to learn on their own and make predictions in unknown scenarios as well. Therefore, the model is restricted to figure out the hidden structure and information in unlabeled data without any kind of external support.

Clustering and association are the two main categories of unsupervised learning. In clustering problems, we are required to find the inherent groupings in the datasets whereas for the association rule learning problems, we have to discover rules which describe large portions of data and other similar relevant information.

Reinforcement Learning

Reinforcement learning is a type of machine learning which can learn from its experience and has the ability to make decisions for completing a given task. In case the training set is not available, reinforcement learning models can make appropriate relations and derive accurate decisions on their own. The model is widely used in the development of machines and software to find the best possible path or behavior for a complex situation. The model keeps on learning and will return to a state in which the user will decide to punish or reward the model, depending upon the quality of output.

As compared to supervised learning, reinforcement learning is based on making decisions sequentially and is dependent upon the state of current and next input. On the other hand, the decision for supervised learning is made on input given at either the start or end state.

Difference Between Supervised and Unsupervised Learning

Supervised and unsupervised learning models are an essential part of machine learning and artificial intelligence models. As both of these learning approaches are different from each other, there are several other factors that make them unique. In supervised learning, the input data uses labeled and known data as input and is usually more complex. Furthermore, it has known number of classes and uses off-line analysis for real-time processing. The accuracy and reliability for supervised machine learning models is higher.

On the other hand, unsupervised machine learning models utilize unknown data as input and have less computational complexity. The number of classes are unknown in the data provided to unsupervised machine learning models. Apart from these differences, the unsupervised learning approach can be used to achieve reliable and moderate accurate results.

Algorithms

Artificial intelligence is the concept of building agents that can derive conclusions and make predictions. To make this happen, data scientists and machine learning engineers have to implement various algorithms and theorems in computing systems to make them intelligent. In machine learning, we can consider an algorithm as a set of rules which are given to an artificial intelligence program to make it learn on its own. Furthermore, intelligent systems are supposed to work without human involvement for which they take support from algorithms.

Neural network or any other machine can only work intelligently if it is provided with proper training data and information. Machine learning models have the power to act and make decisions without being explicitly programed which actually makes them intelligent. An algorithm is a step-by-step technique of solving a problem and is commonly used for mathematical operations, data processing, and other computer operations.

Functions of algorithms are to process information, manipulate data in different ways, and search for a specific item. The main features of an algorithm are explained as follows:

- The aim of an algorithm is to achieve a specific output for each input value.
- An algorithm is based on several continuous steps which might also be repeated to achieve the desired results.
- Once the output is achieved, the algorithm is responsible for finishing the process.

Types of Algorithms

There are three main types of algorithms: sequence, branching, and loop. A sequence algorithm is based on a series of steps and each step is executed one after another to achieve the output. The branching algorithms are represented by conditional if-then problems. In case the condition is true, the algorithm will yield output A whereas in case of false condition, the resultant output shall be B. This category of algorithm is also known as "selection type" algorithm.

Loop is the third type of algorithm. It allows the process to be repeatedly executed upon specific conditions and works on "for" and "while" problems only. Unless the process is complete and the condition is satisfied, loop algorithm will keep on repeating the steps. The following chart shows the working of a simple conditional loop with else-if statements:

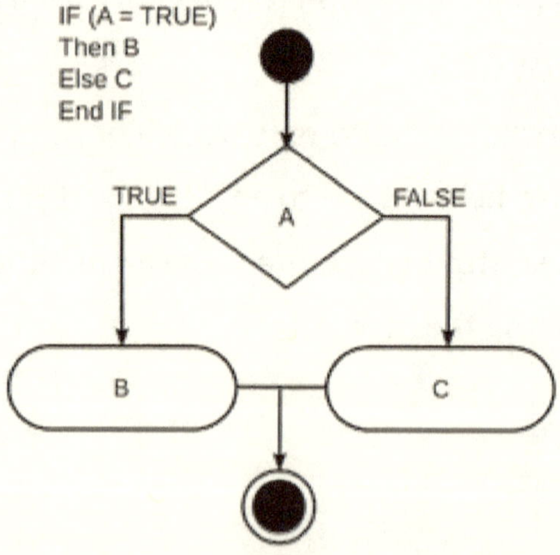

Algorithms are also considered rules that tell computers how to finish processes and help in making decisions as well. Machine learning is the approach through which artificial intelligence uses algorithms to work over various AI functions.

Neural Networks

Neural networks give artificial intelligence the ability to solve complex problems. Since these networks are designed similarly to the human brain and nervous system, data scientists and machine learning engineers can develop high performing AI systems that work similarly to a human brain. Neural networks, deep learning, and artificial intelligence represent powerful and exciting machine learning based techniques that are best suited for solving real world problems. Although no computer could ever achieve the level of human intelligence, AI models based on decision making, inference, and reasoning models can deliver great outcomes and accurate predictions.

How Does a Neural Network Work?

Similar to a human brain, neural networks have the capability to make decisions and make predictions which are best suited for the given dataset. They interpret sensory data by using machine learning perceptions and clustering of raw input. Furthermore, the patterns recognized by neural networks are contained in vectors and are usually numerical. Input data for neural networks can include real world data such as text files, images, audio, video, or graphical files. Each type of data is translated into an understandable format by the neural networks so that relevant operations could be done without any hassle.

Moreover, neural networks are based on classification and clustering models which make it easier for machine learning models to achieve better data insights. Neural networks help to manage unlabeled data by reviewing the similarities within the inputs. After the review is done, the model classifies data and ends up with a labeled dataset to train on. For example, if we want to develop a network which identifies cats, the initial training should include a series of pictures of cats from each angle. As each input is given with a matching identification, such as animals or not animals, the model can differentiate and deliver accurate predictions without any hassle.

To make determinations and defining rules, the decision of each node is sent to the next tier and the process is dependent upon the inputs from the previous tier. Neural networks are based on genetic algorithms, gradient based training, Bayesian methods, and Fuzzy logic theorems.

Types of Neural Networks in AI

The main components of a neural network are input layers, output layers, and hidden layers. Hidden layers are present between the input and output layers which define relationships between the data and also help machine learning models to generate data insights and predictions in a better way. Neural networks are associated with deep learning because of forward and backward propagation of data within the tiers.

Here are the major types of neural networks briefed in detail:

Feed Forward Neural Networks

The feed forward neural networks are the base version of a neural network and they have the responsibility to pass information through different input nodes. To achieve the output node, the process is repeated multiple times and it has the power to process large amounts of data without any interruption. Furthermore, feed forward neural networks are used in the development of major artificial intelligence technologies such as computer vision and facial recognition. As compared to other types of neural networks, feed forward neural networks are simple to operate and yield effective results as well.

Recurrent Neural Networks

Recurrent neural networks have the capability to save the output from processing nodes and return the results back to the model. Since they are complex, in comparison to feed forward networks, data scientists and machine learning engineers use this type of neural network to solve complex problems. Each node in the recurrent neural network model is considered as a memory cell and is responsible for completing the implementation and continuity of operations.

The process of data handling includes the re-use of outputs and in case the network is unable to deliver correct inputs, the system starts to learn on its own and continues to provide accurate predictions during the back propagation.

Convolutional Neural Networks

The convolutional neural networks use different perceptron and have more than one layer connected with each other. Furthermore, these layers are responsible for creating future maps or information related to data so that it could be further broken down for non-linear processing. Convolutional neural networks are mostly used for the development of advanced artificial intelligence applications such as text digitization, facial recognition, and natural language processing.

On the other hand, deconvolutional networks work completely opposite of convolutional neural networks. They are supposed to find lost signals or features that are ranked as unimportant by a convolutional network.

Modular Neural Networks

Modular neural networks have multiple neural networks that work separately from each other. Moreover, the networks do not communicate in any case and never interfere in the activities of other neural networks.

Benefits of Using Artificial Neural Networks

Artificial neural networks are best suited to store information through the entire network and have parallel processing abilities as well. This makes it easier for artificial neural networks to perform multiple tasks at a time without compromising on performance and efficiency. Furthermore, they have the ability to model complex relationships and learn from non-linear datasets by defining relationships between the input and output data. Neural networks do not have any restrictions for input variables and they can be distributed in different patterns as well.

Neural networks are widely implemented in the development of various artificial intelligence and machine learning models.

Popular neural network applications are language generation, translation, and natural language processing systems. Chat bots, stock market prediction, route planning, and optimizing systems are also developed through neural networks.

Chapter 3: Expert Systems and Neural Networks

Expert systems are computer-based decision making and interactive systems which are dependent upon heuristics and facts for solving complex problems. The highest level of human expertise and intelligence can be found in expert systems because they are designed to solve complex issues.

Functionality of Expert Systems

Artificial intelligence and machine learning are concerned with the development of systems which showcase intelligent behavior and work similar to human intelligence. These systems are capable of thinking and predicting through symbolic processing, non-algorithmic processing, and training. Expert systems are capable of deriving solutions to specific problems and assist humans in decision-making as well. Furthermore, expert systems are best suited for advising, diagnosing, and explaining problems. For best performance, the model also predicts results and justifies conclusions to make sure that the output is accurate in each case.

Parts of Expert Systems

The main components of expert systems are knowledge base, inference engine, and user interface. User interface is the most critical part of an expert system because it has to process the user's query and pass it over to the inference engine. Once the information is completely readable, it can be used to display results and communicate with the expert systems as well. Inference engine, on the other hand, is considered as the most vital part of an expert system because it has the rules used to solve the given problem. Inference engine selects the facts and rules for providing answers to the problem and it refers to the knowledge availed from the knowledge base.

Understanding Knowledge

Knowledge is the information achieved from data and is based on past experience and data as well. The components of knowledge include factual knowledge and heuristic knowledge. In factual knowledge, the information is simply accepted by the scholars and engineers of the specific domain whereas in the case of heuristic knowledge, the decisions are dependent upon accurate judgement, practice, and guessing.

The performance of every expert system is dependent upon the accuracy, completeness, and quality of the information which is present in the knowledge base. The knowledge base is comprised of readings from experts, knowledge engineers, and scholars as they are well aware about the topic and can perform an in-depth case analysis as well. Information for knowledge-based systems can be acquired through interviewing, recordings, or accurate findings.

Inference Engine

Inference engine is the best available solution which provides accurate rules and efficient procedures to work on expert systems. For the knowledge based expert systems, inference engine is used to acquire and manipulate information or knowledge from the knowledge base. Furthermore, inference engine makes use of forward chaining and backward chaining to accomplish complex tasks. Inference engine also directs user interface to provide any information that is required for inferencing later.

During the process, the facts from a given case are fed into the working memory in the inference engine. Working memory can also be used as a blackboard and has the capability to process knowledge about the case as well. To achieve a goal state, inference engine repeatedly applies the rules to working memory and also adds new information if required.

Forward Chaining

Forward chaining is a data driven approach and the inferencing process achieves the goal by manipulating given facts. In the knowledge base, each condition of a rule is matched with the facts which are present in the working memory. If several rules match at a single time, a conflict resolution procedure is started by the inference engine. Forward chaining systems are generally used to solve complex problems.

Backward Chaining

In backward chaining, the inference engine makes an attempt to match the conclusion or goal that is assumed by the inference engine. If the hypnotized or assumed goal cannot be supported by premises, then the system will be bound to prove another goal state. Until a goal state is achieved, backward chaining process reviews conclusions that can be supported by the promises.

Characteristics

Expert systems have the highest level of efficiency and expertise. These systems provide improved imaginative problem solving and accuracy as compared to other artificial intelligence models. Furthermore, an expert system has to be reliable and not make any kind of mistakes so that it can deliver on time. The capability to handle challenging decisions and problems make expert systems best suited for designing high performance information systems that are capable of performing complex tasks without any hassle.

To build an expert system, we are required to determine the characteristics of the problem and this task can be best performed by a domain expert or a knowledge engineer. The knowledge engineer will translate knowledge into computer understandable language so that the reasoning structure and inference engine can utilize the knowledge when needed. Furthermore, knowledge engineers will also have to determine the integrated use of uncertain knowledge during the reasoning process.

Comparing Expert Systems with a Conventional System

In a conventional system, processing and knowledge work together and the system is only operational once it is developed completely. Moreover, there is a step by step execution or each part of the algorithm and the system requires full information. For expert systems, the processing mechanism and knowledge database are two separate components and the system can also be launched with a small number of rules. Execution in expert systems is done heuristically and logically whereas the system can perform with both sufficient and insufficient information.

Although expert systems are efficient and reliable, they still have some limitations like every computer machine. Expert system does not have a decision-making power similar to humans and cannot possess human capabilities in any case. Furthermore, the system cannot produce accurate results from less knowledge and needs excessive training to yield the best outputs. Expert systems have received significant improvements through which data scientists and knowledge engineers have become able to develop high performing and reliable information systems.

Applications

Artificial intelligence and expert system models are used together to develop applications and information systems for various industries and businesses. In process control systems, we are required to control physical processes through efficient monitoring for which expert systems are the best option to be considered. Other applications of expert systems include knowledge domain, monitoring systems, design domain, and finance commerce.

Deep Learning

Deep learning is an artificial intelligence and machine learning technique which guides computers about performing specific tasks and works in similar ways to human beings. The technology was originally inspired by the function and structure of the human brain which is also known as artificial neural networks. Deep learning is also considered as an artificial intelligence function which has the capability to create patterns and process data to be used in decision making. Moreover, the model is named as a subset of machine learning in artificial intelligence that features networks which are capable of learning through unsupervised and unlabeled data.

Data gathered from external resources such as social media, e-commerce platforms, Internet search engines, and computer databases is also known as big data. Deep learning models undergo extensive training for which data scientists feed the system with big datasets so that they are able to make accurate predictions and insights in the future. Artificial intelligence systems are increasingly adopting big data and deep learning theories as they greatly help in training the information system within a short period of time.

Why Is Deep Learning Important?

Today, businesses and industries are in need of computing systems and intelligent machines that are able to automate processes and yield accurate predictions for the future. This is only possible if the machine learning or artificial intelligence model is completely trained and can handle any complex scenario without any hassle. Before starting with developing machine learning models, we are required to properly understand the requirements and select the best suitable algorithm and deep learning model to design the system.

Deep learning needs large amounts of labeled data so that it can make the model capable of making accurate decisions in any scenario. Taking the example of autonomous vehicles, data scientists have to make sure that the model is trained for any consequences because of human safety concerns.

Working of Deep Learning models

Deep learning models achieve better recognition and accuracy as compared to other artificial intelligence models. In order to achieve the best outcomes, we are required to feed the deep learning models with high quality datasets which are completely labeled and have their relationships properly defined. Furthermore, processing large amounts of labeled data requires fine computing power and high-performance GPUs. By using high performing GPUs, data scientists are able to reduce training time for deep learning models and achieve better results as well.

Machine Learning and Deep Learning

Machine learning and deep learning are both amazing artificial intelligence techniques that are used to process big data and work through a predefined algorithm to yield accurate results. Deep learning is a subset of machine learning and can take benefit from artificial neural networks to accomplish the process of machine learning. Furthermore, the artificial neural networks work similarly to a human brain because the neuron nodes are interconnected with each other.

Deep learning artificial intelligence has the capability to learn from both unlabeled and unstructured data. Moreover, the approach is best suited for complex problems such as handwriting recognition and object recognition. As it has the power to learn through multiple layers of representation, it can also be used in the automatic feature extraction process without any guidance.

Artificial Neural Networks (ANNs)

Artificial neural networks, or ANNs, are information processing models that are based on the design and pattern of human nervous systems. By using the mathematical model of the brain, data scientists and artificial intelligence engineers design artificial neural networks that have the capability to accomplish complex tasks and processes with high accuracy. ANNs can be used for a variety of tasks and is majorly considered for developing classification models. The method is commonly used in the development of self-driving vehicles, image recognition, and stock market prediction applications.

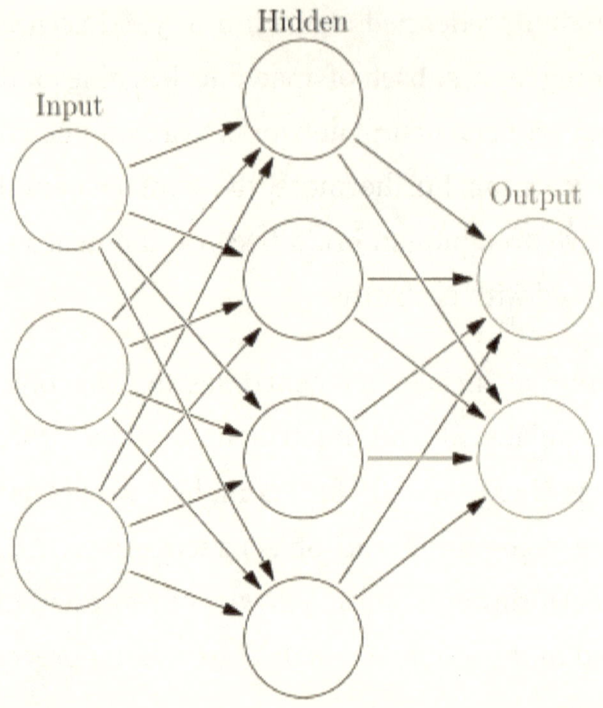

Before starting with the development of artificial neural networks, it is mandatory to learn how they actually learn and what makes them so effective. Information in a neural network flows in two ways. Firstly, when the model is being trained and secondly after the model has been trained properly. The patterns or other vital information taken from the dataset is fed into the network through input neurons which are comprised of different hidden neurons. Once the training process is done, the saved information is sent to the output neurons. This approach is also known as a feedforward network because every neuron receives information from its neighboring neurons. Once the connections are complete, every neuron adds up the collected inputs and in case the threshold of final data is more than a specific value, the neurons will automatically fire the other neurons it is connected with.

How Do Anns Learn?

Artificial neural networks learn from experience and characteristics of training data. By utilizing the feedback from output, ANNs decide what is wrong and right. The element of feedback allows the model to learn things in the same way as a backpropagation process would learn. The network usually performs supervised learning tasks by building knowledge from datasets. Cost function technique is implemented in artificial neural networks to modify initial outputs. These outputs are generally based on the degree to which they are different from their target values. After the process is complete, the results for cost function are returned back across all connections and neurons to adjusts the weights and biases. This pushback approach is also known as backpropagation in artificial neural networks.

Remember that artificial neural networks are divided into separate layers of parallel computing. For each processor in the layer, the number of inputs is multiplied with the original value of weight which is also known as the internal value of operation. Similar to the structure of a biological neuron, artificial neural networks receive multiple inputs and apply various functions and transformations to deliver high quality outputs.

Loss Function

To estimate the loss or error in the outcomes achieved from the artificial neural networks, we can use the loss function feature. Loss function is best suited to measure how good or bad the prediction result was as compared to the correct result. Zero is the ideal cost for artificial neural networks and this can only be achieved without divergence between the expected and estimated value. Therefore, the weights of every interconnected neuron will also be adjusted until the optimum prediction is achieved.

After loss calculation, the information is sent back to the neural network and the process is named backpropagation. However, neurons in the hidden layer will only get a fraction of the total signal loss function because of the relevant contribution given by other neurons. The process is repeated for each layer until each of the neurons in the network has received a loss signal describing their relevant contribution in the total loss.

Gradient Descent

The gradient descent algorithm is best suited to perform optimization in neural networks. Being an iterative optimization algorithm, gradient descent is used to find minimum value for a function which makes it easier to make decisions. To calculate gradient descent, we can use the following equation:

$$J_{m,b} = \frac{1}{N} \sum_{i=1}^{N} (Error_i)^2$$

Gradient optimization can also be used to perform operations through linear regression for which measuring the relationship between heights and weights for the given scenario is compulsory.

Chapter 4: Search Algorithms in Artificial Intelligence

Planning, searching, and evaluation are the main components of artificial intelligence algorithms. Talking about machine learning and deep learning methods, we can notice that there are several algorithms which can increase the performance of models if given high quality training datasets to train on. In artificial intelligence, a search problem is comprised of three main parts defined as follows:

1. State space
2. Start state
3. Goal test

In a state space, there is a set of all possible states given whereas the start state guides the algorithm from where to begin with processing. In the goal test, we can notice a function that checks the current state and returns based on whether the achieved state is a goal state or not. The solution to any search problem is achieved through a sequence of actions which is also known as the plan. For efficient results, we are required to follow the plan throughout the process of search algorithms.

Search in artificial intelligence is also known as the process of moving from a start state to a goal state by completing or transitioning through the intermediate states. At first, we must learn how to define a problem in artificial intelligence. The following terms can be used for the formulation of a problem in AI:

- State: From the initial state, the agent starts, and all of the other states are approachable from the initial state through a sequence of actions or any other possible states.
- Transition: Transition is the process of moving between two or more states.
- Actions: Covers all of the actions which can be executed by an agent. In the action space, a complete list of actions is also provided which an agent can perform in a specific state.
- Search space: Search space is comprised of multiple states in which an agent can move.
- Transition model: A transition model describes results of each action which have occurred in a particular state.

Types of Search Algorithms

To model the sequence of actions during the search procedure, a search is constructed having an initial rate as the root. Each action taken by the search algorithm is used to create branches and results in nodes for those actions. Remember that each node has a unique depth and path cost because it is directly associated from the state space. In searching, the nodes are moved from an unexplored region to an explored region through a strategic order. Moves of the node are also considered as node expansion because there are different search strategies evaluated along with time complexity, completeness, optimality, and space complexity.

The two main categories of search in artificial intelligence are uninformed search and informed search.

Uninformed Search

Uninformed search is a part of general-purpose search algorithms. These algorithms work in a brute force manner and do not have any kind of additional information about the search space or state in the search procedure. Following are the major types of uninformed search strategies:

- Breadth-first search
- Depth-first search
- Depth-limited search
- Iterative deepening depth-first search
- Uniform-cost search

Breadth-First Search

Breadth-first search (BFS) algorithm in artificial intelligence provides the shortest path to achieve a specific solution. As we are required to start searching through each node to identify the root node, breadth-first search is the best strategy for traversing a graph or a tree. Furthermore, this algorithm searches in a breadthwise manner and begins with the root node and then expands through each of the successor nodes. Breadth-first search algorithm can also be implemented by using the First In First Out (FIFO) approach in a queue data structure.

A BFS algorithm will give a solution if it exists and in case there are more than one solution available for a specific problem, then the algorithm will deliver the minimal solution which requires the least number of steps. Although breadth-first search is the finest search algorithm in artificial intelligence, it requires a lot of extra memory because each level of the tree has to be saved into the memory before expanding towards the next level.

Here is a simple example of a BFS algorithm in artificial intelligence:

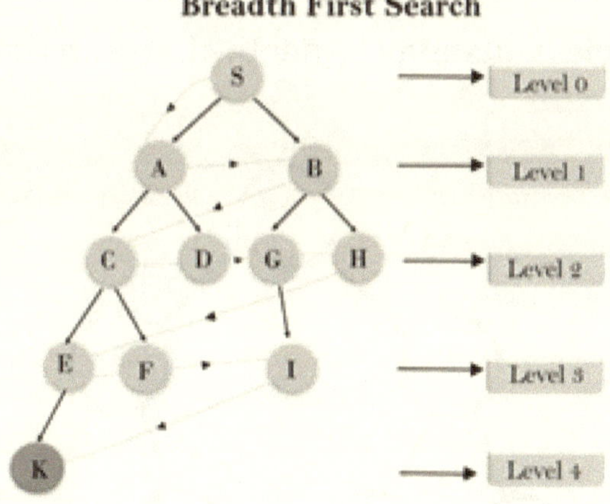

Optimal Path: S--> A--> B--> C--> D--> G--> H--> E--> F--> I-> K

In the above sample tree, we can notice that the traversing is done by using a BFS algorithm. A BFS algorithm starts the searching process from root node S and reaches the goal node K by traversing through layers and will only follow the path shown by using dotted arrows. The total number of nodes created in a worst case can be represented as follows:

b1+b2+b3+b4+b5....+bd.

Depth-First Search

Depth-first search (DFS) algorithm is based on the Last In First Out (LIFO) approach and is implemented in stack data structures as well. The algorithm creates the same number of nodes like the BFS method but only in a different order. Nodes in the depth-first search algorithm on the single path are stored in every iteration from root node to the leaf node. The following tree shows implementation of a depth-first search algorithm:

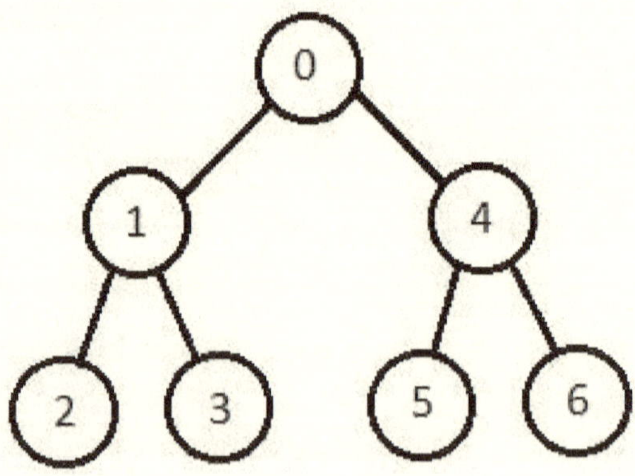

Complexity of the DFS algorithm is dependent upon the number of paths. The algorithm is unable to check for duplicate nodes and is best suited for deep graphs. Progress of DFS starts from the first child node of the search tree and goes deeper until the desired node is found or there are no mode child nodes in the tree.

Depth-Limited Search

Depth-limited search (DLS) algorithm is used to solve the unbounded tree problem in depth-first search. By setting a limit for depth in the tree, the depth-limited search can easily solve the infinite path problem in any search tree.

Iterative Deepening Depth-First Search

Iterative deepening depth-first search algorithm starts with the depth-first search from level one and executes the DFS to level 2. In this way, the search is continued in the tree until the desired solution is found. Moreover, the stacks of nodes are saved automatically and it never creates a node until each of the lower nodes are completely generated. Iterative deepening depth-first search algorithm finishes when it finds the desired solution at depth D. For example:

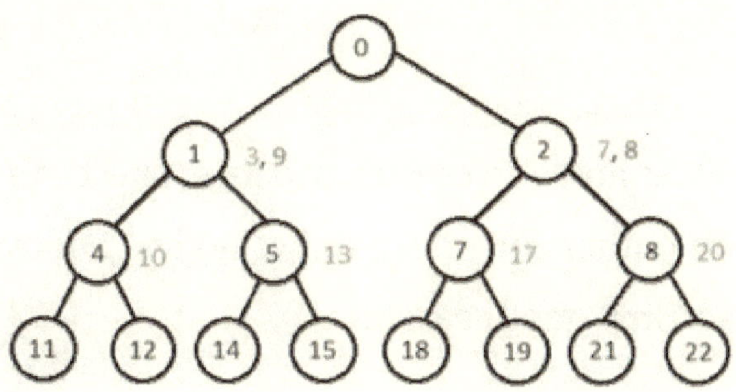

Uniform-Cost Search

The uniform-cost search algorithm performs sorting by increasing the cost path to a node and it only expands the available least cost node. The goal of the uniform-cost search algorithm is to find a path which has the lowest cumulative sum cost. Uniform-cost search is different from breadth-first search and depth-first search because it is based on cost for every traversal in the tree. The aim of uniform-cost search is to find a path which has the lowest cumulative sum of costs.

Informed Search

Informed search algorithms in artificial intelligence have complete information regarding the goal state and it can be obtained through a heuristic as well. This type of search algorithm makes use of domain knowledge and provides more efficient searching as compared to the uninformed search algorithms. In informed search, the algorithms use a heuristic function to estimate the distance of a node to the goal. A heuristic function performs evaluations and helps to calculate cost for each move in the search tree.

The pure heuristic search expands the nodes as per their heuristics values and also creates two lists; one for the expanding nodes and the other for unexpanded nodes. Following are the major types of informed search:

- Best-first search
- A* search

Best-First Search

Best-first search is also known as greedy search and is a type of informed search in artificial intelligence. It is a combination of breadth-first and depth-first search algorithms and uses both search and heuristic function. Through this algorithm, we can select the most promising node and expand the node which is nearest to the goal node. Furthermore, cost for the closest node can also be estimated through a heuristic function as defined below:

$f(n) = g(n)$

$h(n)$ is the total estimated cost from n node to the goal.

Working

Step 1: Begin with traversing the root node.

Step 2: Traverse the neighbor of the root node (left or right) and keep a smaller distance from the root node. Insert the values in ascending order to begin with the queue.

Step 3: After one neighbor node has traversed, take the next neighbor node and repeat step 2.

Step 4: Continue with the process until the goal node is achieved.

At first, the algorithm will place the root node or starting node into the queue and in case the queue is empty, it will stop and return a failure statement. Next, if the first element in the queue is a goal node, the process will stop and return a success statement. If both of these cases do not occur, remove the first element from queue and expand it to calculate the estimated distance to achieve the goal specifically for each child. Moreover, add child nodes in the queue in an ascending order along with the goal distance.

A heuristic can be defined through the following statements:

- H(x) – Estimate of distance of node x from goal node.
- A node is closer to the goal node having a smaller h(x) value.

Example:

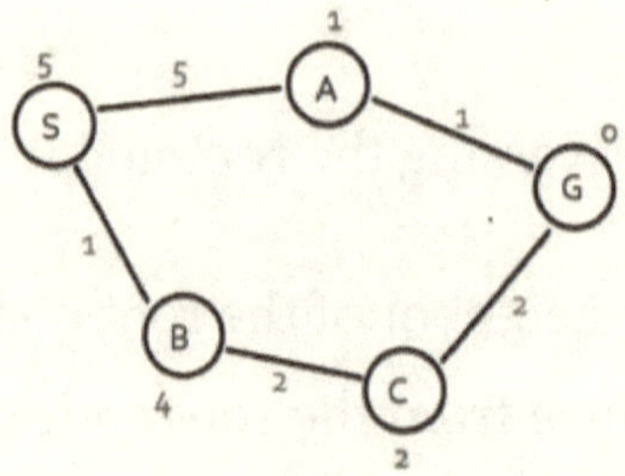

In the best-first search example above, the numbers on the lines traveling from each circle represent actual cost whereas the numbers above and below the circles are heuristic function values. To find a best search path from node S to node G, we can get S->A->G path through the heuristic function. This example shows a simple implementation of a best-first search algorithm in artificial intelligence.

A* Search

A* search is a combination of best fit search and uniform-cost search. This algorithm is a popular way to graph traversals and path finding in search trees. Whenever the A* search algorithm enters a state, it will calculate the cost f(n) and will travel to all of the other neighboring nodes as well. At last, it will enter the node which has the lowest f(n) value. The values can be calculated by using the following formula:

f(n) = g(n) + h(n)

g(n) is the value for shortest path from start node to 'n' node whereas h(n) is a heuristic approximation of node value. Remember that the efficiency of A* search is dependent upon the heuristic value or h(n) value. By reviewing the type of search problem, we can select different heuristics functions to reach the optimal solution.

A* search algorithm works in the following steps:

Step 1: Place start node in the open list and check whether it is empty or not. If the open list is empty, just stop and return failure.

Step2: Choose the node from the open list having the lowest evaluation function (g+h) value. In case the node n is a goal node, just stop and return success.

Step 3: Expand node n and place all of the successors. For each successor, check whether it is present in the open or closed list.

Step 4: If the node n is present in the open and closed list, it should be linked back to the pointer which has the lowest g(n) value.

Step 5: Return back to step 1.

A* search algorithm yields the fastest search results as compared to other search algorithms in artificial intelligence. Furthermore, this algorithm can solve complex problems with better accuracy and efficiency.

Heuristic Search

Heuristic is an approach to solve a specific problem faster than the conventional search methods. Most often, complex search problems are difficult to solve with the help of classic methods and formulas. With a heuristic function, a search algorithm can identify the shortest and least cost path in a search tree without any hassle. Although the approach is not feasible for every search problem, we can still use heuristic functions in different ways to achieve a desired goal.

In artificial intelligence, there are two major types of heuristic techniques known as direct heuristic search and weak heuristic search. Uninformed search, blind control strategy, and blind search are the most popular direct search techniques in artificial intelligence. To complete the operation, the model has to search the complete state space and derive a solution that is capable of performing multiple tasks. Another name for informed search is heuristic control strategy. These are weak heuristic search techniques in which each node has a unique heuristic function.

Hill Climbing

Hill climbing is a heuristic approach for optimizing problems through mathematical functions. It makes use of greedy approach to solve problems and the model keeps on generating possible solutions until the best outcome is achieved. By using inputs of a heuristic function, hill climbing solves problems where we are required to minimize or maximize a real function by selecting values from given inputs.

Features

This artificial intelligence algorithm has two components known as state and value. Hill climbing is used to produce feedback which helps in deciding the final direction of moving within the search space. Greedy approach in hill climbing search moves in the direction which has minimal cost and it does not backtrack the search space in any case because it is unable to remember previous covered states.

Different regions in state space landscape are local maximum, global maximum, current state, flat local maximum, and shoulder. Local maximum is the state which is better in performance as compared to its neighboring states. In the global maximum region, the best possible state of state space is covered and it has the highest value for the objective function. Current state is present in a landscape diagram whereas the flat local maximum is a flat scape in landscape which includes all neighboring states of current states with the same value. Furthermore, shoulder is a plateau region that has an uphill edge in the search state.

Types of Hill Climbing

Here are the three main types of hill climbing algorithms in artificial intelligence:

Simple Hill Climbing

Simple hill climbing is the most popular way of using the hill climbing algorithm. In this category, the algorithm only evaluates neighbor node state and selects the one which best optimizes the current cost. Furthermore, it sets the resultant node as the current state. Simple hill climbing is less time-consuming but does not guarantee solution in each operation.

At first, simple hill climbing evaluates the initial state and in case it is the goal state, it returns a success statement and stops the operation. The loop is continued until a solution is found and the algorithm automatically applies an operator to the existing state. Next, the algorithm checks for a new state and in case the selected node is not better than the current state, it will repeat the whole process to yield optimum results.

Steepest Ascent Hill Climbing

In steepest ascent hill climbing search, the algorithm determines all of the neighboring nodes of current states and chooses the one which is nearest to the goal state. To start the operation, the initial state is evaluated and the loop continues until the desired solution is found. Moreover, there are separate rules which apply to each operator in the search and how to generate the best suited results.

Stochastic Hill Climbing

Stochastic hill climbing randomly selects one neighbor and does not check one separately before moving further.

Chapter 5: Artificial Intelligence and Business

With the evolvement of the Internet and digital tools, business activities and operations have received significant improvements. Artificial intelligence and machine learning are the main components of automated processes because these methodologies have brought unprecedented possibilities and breakthroughs. Moreover, simulation of human intelligence in computer machines have minimized the need for manpower because of automation and prediction facilities.

Although artificial intelligence has certain limitations, it can be programed to learn, self-correct, and reason to make further accurate decisions. Furthermore, AI has increased the growth factor for businesses and enabled companies to address weaknesses, improve their performance, and bring better outcomes within a short period of time.

How Do Businesses Use AI?

Artificial intelligence is widely implemented in business systems such as data analytics, automation, natural language processing, and prediction. With improved efficiencies and performance, machine learning and artificial intelligence have greatly revolutionized the work procedure in industries and companies.

Automation is a process which allows an organization to carry on its routine activities without the need of human intervention. Because intelligent machines have the capability to make decisions and bring accurate predictions for the future, they are likely to bring positive outcomes for each industry.

In most businesses, artificial intelligence is the main driving force behind everyday activities and tasks. To make things more effective, we are required to select the AI methodologies and techniques after proper search and evaluation because every method is not suitable for each business. This is because of the major differences in data and information that is being fed into the knowledge systems of a business.

Where to Start?

At first, overview your business requirements and other major factors such as security, efficiency, performance, and reliability. Some businesses want to improve customer experience whereas others want to focus on increasing profit rates. There are several tasks which are repetitive and can create problems for employees to complete the same activity each day. But to succeed with artificial intelligence, an effective strategy must be a part of your business plan. Even if you are completely unaware about how artificial intelligence works, getting support from an experienced data scientist can prove to be of great support.

Artificial intelligence can do amazing activities but only if it is implemented in the correct manner. Training of AI and machine learning models differentiates it from other traditional software applications such as data analysis. To achieve the best results, you will need loads of high-quality training data. In case you find it difficult to train your artificial intelligence model, it will definitely affect the overall performance and prediction results for your business. Furthermore, identify the potential signals in your data and measure results in advance. This approach will greatly help you in achieving long term advantages out of your AI business model.

Most companies with the determination to implement artificial intelligence and machine learning models into their business lack the best data handling practices. The artificial intelligence team is basically comprised of a data scientist, a data engineer, and a software engineer. A data engineer has the task to organize information whereas a data scientist will investigate the information that is to be used for AI model training. Once both the data engineers and data scientists are done with their tasks, a software engineer will take over the project and implement the AI system for the specific company or business.

Collecting Training Data

Performance of a machine learning and artificial intelligence model is directly linked with training data. Once the data has been collected, artificial intelligence can be applied to achieve certain insights and improvements. Training data has predefined attributes and relationships which enable the AI system to improve with time. When the workplace data is reviewed and analyzed, data scientists have to gain insights before assigning any employee a specific task. Data analysis must also highlight the main areas in which employees of a certain organization need improvement so that the best suitable AI system could be suggested.

Furthermore, analyzing training data also gives information about the type of training material to be used based on the learning styles of the employees. The process of collecting and analyzing data from different employees is supposed to be continuous in order to keep the system updated and performing well. Companies need to understand that training can greatly affect the performance of their information systems and applications. On the other hand, the results of your application will be biased in case the training data which is used to train the AI model is biased.

Learning and Development

Learning and development insights are the best techniques to improve predictive capacities and performance of a machine learning model. By using positive insights, an organization will be able to develop a better understanding of learning behavior as well. Most importantly, artificial intelligence solutions will keep on improving due to the development of machine learning algorithms and researches which are performed by data scientists. Virtual mentoring is an advanced artificial intelligence technique that is used for tracking the learning process and also evaluates essential steps that are required to train the model effectively. This process also covers advanced domain understanding and evaluation of programs that are used to optimize the performance of AI models.

Traditional learning and development techniques have brought significant disadvantages to the business and corporate sector. Some of the major factors include limited library of content because most of the learning and development tools are using long format training modules like PowerPoint presentations. This approach limits the freshness and variety of learning content in different ways. Furthermore, these systems are not user-friendly and are also not suited for the digital workforce.

Application of Artificial Intelligence in Business

Artificial intelligence has several uses in the business and corporate sector. Along with providing new opportunities to complete routine tasks, AI systems bring long term growth and development as well. We can use artificial intelligence technologies for improving customer services such as virtual assisted programs and automated billing tools. Artificial intelligence is widely used for increasing manufacturing efficiency and output. For example, an automated production line featuring industrial robots can learn to perform mundane or labor-intensive tasks.

Predictive performance artificial intelligence models are best suited for reaching performance goals. Moreover, AI is widely used for predictive behavior tools in detecting credit card fraud. To meet the increasing demand for automated systems, data scientists and machine learning engineers are working to bring new features and facilities in artificial intelligence models. Apart from bringing improvements, developers are working to make AI models reliable, efficient, and safe as well.

Developing AI strategy

Businesses can avail long term advantage from artificial intelligence strategies. To make this happen, it is compulsory to focus on your goals, requirements, and start after proper research and evaluation has been done. Completing the artificial intelligence use case template for your business and defining priorities of tasks will help in achieving strategic objectives. Furthermore, some common ways to use artificial intelligence are to develop more intelligent products and make businesses processes smarter by adding intelligent services. Automating the manufacturing process and repetitive business tasks are also essential parts of AI use case development. With the help of artificial intelligence use cases, you can start to rank your projects to overview performance and priority levels. Once the AI strategy template is complete, demonstrating possible ideas and requirements becomes simple.

Technology and infrastructure are the core parts of artificial intelligence model development. Furthermore, it also helps companies in identifying what technology they will be needing in each layer which includes collecting data, storing data, processing data, and communicating insights from data.

Improving Workplace Learning with AI

Learning in artificial intelligence models is the best approach to make information systems capable of delivering accurate insights and predictions. Along with the process of learning, AI will help the employees of any company to learn and complete routine activities without any hassle. This process is accomplished by integrating employee training and workflow together through which we can also analyze workplace behavior.

At first, we have to focus on the development of personalized learning pathways. This step is based on the concept that not the same training is suitable for each employee. With the help of machine learning and artificial intelligence, learning and development models can easily understand behaviors and predict suitable results as well. Depending on external variables such as job roles, previous learning experiences, educational background, and learning styles, data scientists are able to develop high performance machine learning models.

Reinforced Learning

Employees participating in training sessions and tutorials can learn the best practices for using and implementing AI models. By learning simple relations between variables and attributes of training data, employees can enhance the speed at which they accomplish routine tasks and yield better results in a short period of time. It is mandatory to create training content at a high scale for agile businesses which need dynamic requirements. Furthermore, reinforcement learning can also deliver the best content for the information system of any business in order to improve work relationships and bring better outcomes.

Human Interactions

Artificial intelligence and machine learning models are capable of understanding human language. To make the models understand better, a natural language processing approach is used while building machine learning models. In order to achieve better results, businesses and companies are advised to conduct new training sessions often and enforce the need for training. Estimating subject understanding and tracking learner progress are the vital parts of learning and designing machine learning models. Furthermore, artificial intelligence also helps leaders in gaining access to key insights like how employees learn and what are the main aspects which can improve the learning procedure. Companies can also collect data on other factors such as the time needed for respective employees to complete each section.

Removing Bias

Training sessions are the best source to remove bias in learning. Artificial intelligence also represents analysis of data and AI-based systems can share the recommendations which are best suited for the need of an organization and its employees. AI bots are programed to pick up on comments and feedback shared by employees on what they are learning and what they think about the training procedure. Removing bias is an essential part of the employee training process and people can also be encouraged to learn through story line and game-based courses.

Data Collection

With the latest advancements of AI technologies, machine learning is deeply associated with artificial intelligence and in most cases, machine learning is also ranked equal to AI. The concept and theories of machine learning are directly dependent on data to perform supervised, unsupervised, and artificial training. In supervised learning, training of a machine learning model is done by using a sample of labeled class data that allows the model to differentiate between right and wrong decisions. On the other hand, the next approach of learning in machine learning models is unsupervised learning which allows the machine to learn on its without regular guidance.

In both cases, the most essential factor is the learning process and quality of data. No artificial intelligence or machine learning model can yield one-hundred percent accurate results without the availability of labeled training datasets. During the training procedure, machine learning models develop the power to make complex decisions and accurate predictions for any complex scenario. The major steps for the process of data preparation include required data, availability and profiling of data, sourcing data, integrating data, cleaning data, and preparing data for learning.

Mindful Data Collection

To reduce the time preparing the data, we can also consider the practice of mindful data collection. In a typical AI information system, the data is created to perform specific transactions in a system and we are required to follow the practices of mindful data collection to improve results. For implementing mindful data in a machine learning model, we need to review the existing data dictionary and public data standards as well. Moreover, data governance organization and owners of major processes within the organization can utilize the properties of mindful artificial intelligence data collection.

Most of the clients and companies consider data quality as a strategic asset. Data can be collected in the form of videos, text, or images and we can also use the existing data sources to train a system. In machine learning, it is mandatory that the data is properly labeled and has the capability to determine the output of a system. Once the system is working in the correct path, it will automatically start to deliver perfect results and accurate predictions without any need for human interference.

Maintaining Data Quality

Data quality is an essential part of artificial intelligence driven products. At first, determine the type of data which is best suitable for your business and train your model completely. Make sure that there is no repetitive or false data because it will directly affect the performance of your machine learning model. Furthermore, source data responsibly because using pre-labeled data or critical information to train machine learning models can result in future problems. For supervised learning models, it is mandatory that you have proper labels for your data.

After you are done with the process of data collection, the next step is to interpret the machine learning output to make sure that it meets the required standards. If it does not qualify, there might be some serious problems with the data that has been used in training.

Things to Remember

Although artificial intelligence and machine learning models are great performers, we are still required to take care of certain aspects to obtain the best results. After the model selection process is complete, the next part is to get training datasets and add it into the machine learning model. Labeled and high-quality datasets make it easier for the model to analyze trends and relationships in data.

The goal of developing artificial intelligence models is to give a tough time to the competitors. There are thousands of artificial intelligence and machine learning applications that are offering amazing results. To differentiate your project from others, working to add extra features and support will prove to be of great help.

Chapter 6: Use of AI in the Human Resource Department

The ever-increasing number of affordable and robust computing technologies have transformed the way in which operations are performed in corporate departments. Artificial intelligence is bringing unlimited opportunities and facilities for industries through which different tasks can be automated without any hassle. Considering business aspects, artificial intelligence has brought long term improvements in every sector. Furthermore, AI software helps in managing workload and increases efficiency as well.

The human resource (HR) department is the main driving force behind any business and company. Today, HR professionals are focusing to bring new revolutions in hiring processes by optimizing the combination of automated work and employees. Human resource executives and organizational leaders have greatly supported artificial intelligence as a reliable and effective way to manage HR functions.

Evolution of AI in the Human Resource Department

The hiring process is divided into multiple states and HR managers have to follow a predefined format to complete screening, interviewing, testing, and hiring procedures. Companies and industries receive thousands of resumes each day and it often becomes impossible to read each one by one. For most companies, a talent acquisition process is considered the best practice to find the most suitable candidate. Nowadays, companies need significant, immediate, and measurable results to save time and resources to complete the hiring process.

Although interviewing each candidate separate is a difficult task, the final decision depends upon the predefined criteria by a specific company. Here are the main functions which can be performed through artificial intelligence in human resource departments:

Talent Acquisition

Artificial intelligence has brought amazing breakthroughs and improvements on how routine tasks are performed in the corporate sector. The greatest advantage of artificial intelligence models in human resource departments is automated talent acquisition. Although not all stages of recruitment could be done through AI systems, the initial stage can prove to be of great support.

Take for example chatbots. They have the capability to answer routine questions from candidates and also provide relevant guidance. Furthermore, chatbots are the best source of gathering candidate information and also provide support in checking resumes. This eventually speeds up the screening and recruitment process because it takes long hours to read each resume separately. For some companies, the traditional recruitment process is best because they require a specific skill set and usually get a limited number of applications for the job posting.

Furthermore, artificial intelligence also helps in removing human bias because the algorithm only searches for relevant elements that are included in each resume such as experience and skills. Hiring managers can use artificial intelligence applications to look for potential candidates for new job openings. Moreover, the AI augmented software is efficient, reliable, and a convenient source for completing the initial stages of the hiring process.

Training of Employees

The human resource department is also responsible for employee training and improvement. Regular training is an essential part of every company because the employees need to learn the latest techniques and skills to deliver the best outcomes. Large datasets with information on skills and past job profiles are best for e-learning artificial intelligence platforms. E-learning platforms benefit from AI capabilities and improve job-related skills through effective planning, coordinating, and organizing employee training.

The artificial intelligence e-learning platform creates highly organized learning pathways by overviewing employee skills and requirements of the company. E-learning platforms also help the employees in great ways such as the ability to improve their skills and performance in routine activities. Artificial intelligence solves career pathing problems by using the history of an employee, their work experience, and available career paths as well.

Onboarding

Onboarding is an essential part of analyzing an employee's performance, efficiency, and willingness to complete a given task. Onboarding artificial intelligence algorithms have the capability to set up company systems and brief employees regarding tasks, benefits, and job profiles. Identifying possible behavior and identifying repetitive employee questions are also an essential part of the onboarding process.

How Are AI and HR Linked Together?

Artificial intelligence has many branches and models that are exclusively designed for human resource departments. There are many difficulties and problems that need to be handled while designing artificial intelligence systems for HR departments so that companies do not have to compromise in talent acquisition or employee management tasks. These models are usually developed through the theorems and techniques of machine learning, deep learning, and predictive analysis. Human resource management makes use of machine learning and predictive analysis to understand acquisition and talent attrition as well.

Handling of Repetitive Tasks

Human resource managers have to spend a lot of time completing repetitive tasks. This process is complex and resource-consuming as well because employees find it boring to perform the same activity each day. There are several repetitive questions asked to the employees related to leaves, company policies, and reimbursements in routine. To automate these activities, we can take help from artificial intelligence powered tools and get suitable answers without any hassle.

With the support of artificial intelligence, human resource managers need not to spend more time checking routine administrative tasks. These regular and low value processes can be easily automated through artificial intelligence models and allow HR managers to focus on aspects which will bring long term benefit to the organization.

Employee Management

Employees are definitely the most vital asset of any organization. Each year, corporate companies use significant resources to analyze and gather data which can help in evaluating their performance and skills. Although employee management tasks were performed through traditional information systems in the past, now AI bots are capable of handling each activity on their own. Without being explicitly programed, AI bots have the capability of checking through documents and identifying any anomalous or unusual documents. Furthermore, they can also detect change in voices, linguistic cues, and word choices.

To manage core human resource processes, organizations are working with artificial intelligence and machine learning models to perform experiments of different kinds. These experiments include measuring employee engagement, automating onboarding processes, and making automated interviews. Artificial intelligence has to offer tools and customized products to cater the requirements of growing marketplaces. Furthermore, intelligent learning platforms and artificial intelligence recruitment provide long term benefits to companies and help in improving the performance of the human resource department.

In the future, we can expect a strong relation between human resource and natural language processing. This is an artificial intelligence approach through which companies can study resumes and communicate with potential candidates of different languages without any hassle. Furthermore, the potential of this technology is attracting organizations and companies because they can easily conduct research and find the best suitable candidate for the job posting.

Impact of AI in Human Resource

The human resource department, as we learned, is all about recruiting and managing employee activities. The primary benefits of human resource technology include the approach for cost saving and improving efficiency by automating everyday repetitive tasks. Artificial intelligence has brought even bigger outcomes and profitability to businesses of all kinds. Moreover, human resource is getting long term benefits in terms of support in handling administrative tasks without any hassle. To obtain long term benefits, businesses and corporate sector industries can take support form data scientists and machine learning experts. This will make it easier to finish the selection process of AI models for human resource departments and as a result, the company will be able to manage and process routine tasks without any hassle.

Artificial intelligence has the power to make a strong impact in every department and industry. When it comes to the human resource department, hiring managers can automate the candidate screening procedure and sort out hiring problems within no time.

Decision-Making

In artificial intelligence and machine learning models, decision making and prediction results are dependent upon how well the model is trained. Human resource leaders can make better business decisions and improve the workflow by integrating AI into human resource processes. HR technology has different tasks for which decisions have to be made for the best possible outcome for the organization. Intelligent automation capabilities in artificial intelligence machines help in making tough decisions and complete processes with one-hundred percent accuracy.

The main use of artificial intelligence in recruitment is to complete vital tasks such as candidate sourcing, candidate screening, lead nurturing, interviewing, and onboarding. Artificial intelligence is making organizations meet the increasing number of employee expectations. To make this happen, human resource teams work on talent processes and reduce employee turnover rates and build stronger teams. The main areas that are impacted by AI in the human resource department are workforce planning, performance management, career pathing, people analytics, and leadership.

Employee Engagement and Benefits

Businesses need new ways to interact with their employees in order to boost performance and meet work targets. The employee engagement use cases availed through artificial intelligence are real-time feedback platforms, intelligent surveys, personalized communications and messaging, recognition, and rewards. Artificial intelligence and automation also simplify the administration and management of employee benefits. With AI, human resource departments can complete administration tasks such as personalization, automation, compliance, and communication with ease.

Income and Wages

Human resource departments are always in need of improvements. With the support of artificial intelligence models, we can help employees in developing strong skills and abilities to complete routine tasks. Activities such as job replacement and wage loss have greatly affected employees. Due to automation, the need for a human workforce has been reduced which in return has affected companies in different ways. To manage change, human resource departments need to use automation tools effectively so that it does not affect employee income or wages in any case. With the passage of time, HR needs to learn and make sure that decisions are made in the best benefit of every employee. Furthermore, human resource continues to gain a complete understanding of how artificial intelligence impacts their organizations as there is a huge growth in employee experience.

Prediction

The process to assess and predict employee engagement and future turnover is time consuming and requires a lot of hard efforts from the human resource managers. With the development of high-performance artificial intelligence models, HR can provide relevant data and get accurate insights and predictions without any hassle. Deep learning and machine learning models have the capability to predict more quickly and accurately as compared to the traditional computing models. In this regard, HR managers are required to gather high quality information and make sure that there is no repetitive or redundant data included in the training datasets.

Deciding Benefits

Employees of any company expect routine benefits and perks along with their monthly salary. With the help of artificial intelligence, human resource managers can complete the open enrollment process and overview employee performance. In this way, they can easily check the capacity of each employee and decide the benefits that can be given. Artificial intelligence can help employees to determine the coverage on disability benefits and life insurance. Generally, companies have a predefined standard and scale for allowing benefits to the employees but in case they need other coverage, HR can get accurate answers to questions related to medical conditions, insurance coverage, and cost through artificial intelligence systems.

Similarly, the approach also helps in the development of retirement planning modules. Companies can get relevant information from each employee such as living expenses, current pay, and service time in order to determine retirement benefits.

Ways to Use Artificial Intelligence

Before you start with the implementation of artificial intelligence models in your company, make sure that you have performed in-depth research and analysis. Not only will this help in getting the best outcomes but will also reduce the cost of completing routine tasks and increases efficiency rates as well. It is recommended that every ongoing process in the artificial intelligence model is properly documented and well understood.

Furthermore, HR managers can also create a review process of the results availed from the AI model. In order to implement the review process, they can add inclusion and exclusion tests of employees who are selected and also for those who got rejected. Artificial intelligence can save companies money and resources in great ways. This is only possible if the human resource department is working the way it should be and has the capability to hire the right people.

Artificial intelligence can improve compliance and reduce the number of human errors because the technology has the capability to automate most of the repetitive tasks. Remember that repetitive tasks have a high expectation of human errors and might result in data incongruity and noncompliance. Furthermore, the automation of human resources also allows the employees to manage their own learning hours and start activities which are simple and yield better results.

Today, artificial intelligence has started to engage the workforce and is helping employees in managing their time. In return, this adds more strategic and corporate value to the business because HR managers are able to solve complex problems through artificial intelligence models. Previously, it was quite difficult to manage employee and company relationships through traditional information systems because they did not provide real-time updates and proper information regarding the ongoing task. Furthermore, traditional systems were prone to error and were time consuming as compared to the state-of-the-art artificial intelligence models.

Achieving Best Results

Although there is no match in terms of performance, reliability, and efficiency of artificial intelligence models, there are some techniques that can be followed to get better results. Artificial intelligence facilitates human resource departments in great ways and has also created a value proposition in order to achieve a clear business vision. For the human resource process, companies are required to bring some major changes in their work procedure. The initial artificial intelligent pilots in human resource technology need to be leveraged to bring about positive responses within the entire workforce.

As we have learned the concepts of how artificial intelligence models work and search to complete a specific task, following some key steps will surely help in achieving great results within a short period of time. Furthermore, the purpose of artificial intelligence technology is to automate processes and bring long term benefits to the organizations. Improved employee experience and engagement are the main factors behind the success of any company and it should be remembered that the aim of developing artificial intelligence models was to facilitate employee experience.

Software Development with AI

Traditionally, computer programs were required to be explicitly programed and could not perform any extra tasks without human intervention. With the help of artificial intelligence and machine learning programs, we can automate the process and achieve better outcomes without guiding the system. This approach is best suited for people and companies with non-technical backgrounds as they can get accurate insights, predictions, and solve problems in real-time without any hassle. There are several decisions and tasks that have to be performed through artificial intelligence. Machine learning has completely transformed the software development process and has brought new methods to develop, maintain, and upgrade information systems.

Machine learning models can fetch data from different sources because they are iteratively trained to perform multiple tasks at a time. This brings more ease to software engineers and developers because they can implement predefined machine learning modules in the software code. In this way, they can reduce the need for writing long codes and make a system that is capable of solving complex problems without any hassle. The best impact of artificial intelligence and machine learning is in the software development industry because computer programming is the way that humans define, perceive, and execute the software development process.

Software Development Life Cycle

The traditional software development life cycle is divided into multiple steps. The process includes requirement analysis, design, development, testing, deployment, and maintenance. This is completely different from the machine learning model development process and is based on the predefined rules of software development. In the machine learning model development process, the steps covered as mentioned are as follows:

- Problems and goals definition
- Data collection
- Data preparation
- Model engagement
- Model deployment and integration
- Model learning

With the passage of time, machine learning systems have become complex and require multiple dependencies to deliver one-hundred percent results. Moreover, there are several major layers including interfaces and functionality that are directly linked with the software development process. Actually, machine learning models have their own maintenance and debugging challenges due to the real-world problems they have to handle in routine.

AI Software Development Process

Software design is the first step of software development. In software engineering, we are required to plan a project and design it from scratch for which software engineers have to follow the predefined rules of software development. To come up with a high performing and reliable solution, software design is the main area that needs to be focused on. A designer starts the process by overviewing each perspective of the project and the required solutions. Once the designing is complete, the process is further investigated until the requirements are completely satisfied. Setting the right plan and choices for each stage of the software development process can help in achieving the best results and performance in the future. Tools such as the artificial intelligence design assistant are best suited for understanding user requirements and use the obtained knowledge to create the best software and websites for the user.

Testing and Validating

Applications need to perform well in each scenario. For interaction, applications have to undergo different APIs which helps them in improving performance levels with each day. Furthermore, the increase in complexity also results in more challenges that are supposed to be handled by the machine learning and artificial intelligence models. Artificial intelligence tools can also be used to create test information, check information authenticity, and give a better scope for test management. When trained in the right way, artificial intelligence tools can ensure that the system is problem-free and is fully meeting the client's requirements.

Moreover, test engineers do not have to create manual test cases which are time consuming and require a lot of hard efforts as well. With the help of automated AI testing tools, software quality assurance engineers can calculate the performance of the software and make suitable suggestions as well. With automated artificial intelligence testing, we can also increase the overall scope of tests that lead to further improvement of software quality.

Testing GUI

Graphical user interfaces (GUI) deliver simple and attractive opportunities for clients to improve the overall user experience and get a better turnover rate. GUI is more commonly used in the development of critical systems and is responsible for maintaining the reliability and effectiveness of the artificial intelligence software. Although there are very few techniques and tools available to help in improving the testing process, it often becomes difficult for the test engineers to perform tests on GUI programs.

Once the testing is complete, the test designer changes the test suite and begins with re-testing. As a result, the developers are able to identify the loopholes in the system and make suitable changes before implementing the model into the industrial information system.

Strategic Decision-Making

Strategic decision making is an essential part of AI model development. In the past, developers had to perform extensive research and evaluation before adding features into the product, but with the introduction of machine learning models, things have become much easier. Generally, transformation of business processes and requirements into technology specifications need thorough planning and evaluation. Machine learning can help computer programs and software development companies to speed up the process. Furthermore, they can deliver the product in less time and increase revenue as well.

Chapter 7: Artificial Intelligence in Real Life

Understanding the importance and benefits of technology will help businesses to achieve their goals. Artificial intelligence is a major branch of computer science that is used for automating processes and developing accurate prediction models. This process is made possible through learning capabilities of the machine learning technologies. The use of artificial intelligence in organizations, security frameworks, energy, government, and natural resource management is increasing with each day.

Most of the AI and machine learning developers are now working to achieve a basic goal which is to build artificial intelligence models that can take over human workload. Although this is a good approach, it certainly negatively impacts the wages and incomes of employees. With the integration of automated tools and technologies, the need for a human workforce is reducing with each passing day. Furthermore, artificial intelligence has now become a major part of the health and medical industry through which doctors and specialists are able to diagnose and treat any kind of illness with ease. AI is now becoming the norm in a lot of sectors such as automotive, security, finance, virtual assistance, and economy.

Artificial Intelligence and Finance

Risk Management

It often becomes difficult to handle financial tasks due to high security and performance requirements. To begin with implementing artificial intelligence in the financial sector, data scientists and machine learning engineers have to perform in depth research and evaluation. Financial information systems have enormous amounts of data and the system should be capable of handling tons of transactions without any delay. Algorithms designed for the financial sector are highly reliable and are tested to deliver one-hundred percent results in any scenario. Moreover, they can also manage both structured and unstructured data along with quick identification of potential failure causes.

Fraud Detection and Prevention

Artificial intelligence and machine learning models have the capability to detect fraudulent activities and stop unwanted operations in real-time. In recent years, banks and financial institutions have implemented AI models into their systems and databases. Fraud detection systems have the capability to analyze the client's location, behavior, and credit history in real-time.

Other fraudulent activities like money laundering can also be avoided through AI models. Machines are designed to finish alleged money laundering schemes and protect financial and government institutions from any kind of unwanted loss.

Trading

Artificial intelligence and machine learning models are based on the concepts and theories of statistics. Trading is greatly expanding in the stock markets all over the world and traders are getting the best predictions and recommendations through AI tools. Intelligent trading systems have the capability to monitor structured and unstructured databases. In a structured database, we can have information from spreadsheets or other databases whereas in the unstructured category, the information is taken from sources like social media or the news. For faster trading, we are required to make quick decisions which is now possible with AI tools.

Trading algorithms are based on artificial intelligence models to make predictions and calculations depending on the market conditions. Machine learning algorithms are trained on past data and trade history which allows them to make accurate insights and predictions. Moreover, the technology has greatly improved the validation process which has helped traders in getting information regarding the trade without any hassle.

In the banking sector, artificial intelligence powers smart chatbots that provide real-time answers and solutions to the customers. Voice control assistants have now been introduced which get smarter each day and have self-education features as well. There are different AI apps and tools which offer personalized financial advice and support individuals in any financial problem. These intelligent tools can track income, recurring expenses, and calculate spending habits as well. On the other hand, we can also use AI finance tools to obtain an optimized plan and get financial support as well.

Future

In the future, we are about to witness amazing improvements and upbringings in the financial sector. These improvements will be done through artificial intelligence and will get people and the finance industry to benefit greatly. Artificial intelligence is reshaping the business process of finance and commerce industry from which traders and businessmen can get all kinds of support with ease. Furthermore, accounts and transactional security are about to receive major upgrades along with the expansion of cryptocurrency and blockchains. We can also expect improved customer care systems that work through self-help virtual reality systems.

Businesses can use the information delivered by the AI finance tools to overview past sales information and trends that can affect a trade. In this way, both large- and small-scale businesses can achieve their targets and boost the profits in a short period of time. In the event of a bad market scenario, businesses can develop a strong position by studying trade history to get out of problems in an effective way. Artificial intelligence allows companies to keep their inventory efficiently stocked and project managers can easily interpret the data.

Natural Language Processing

The development of natural language processing is based on the theories and models of artificial intelligence. Natural language processing is the ability of a machine learning model to understand human language and is a major part of artificial intelligence. This approach has helped companies and businesses to communicate with people from all over the world in different languages. Human speech is not always precise and every single one of us has a unique linguistic structure. The process of translation is dependent on several major factors like regional dialects, variables, and social context.

Moreover, natural language processing is a way for computers to understand, analyze, and derive accurate meaning from human language in a useful and smart way. Machine learning and artificial intelligence models are designed to perform multiple tasks such as translation, relationship extraction, automatic summarization, topic segmentation, and sentiment analysis.

Natural language is an effective approach to analyze text and allows machines to understand how actually humans speak. This approach is commonly used for machine translation, text mining, and automated question answering.

How Is It Used?

Natural language processing (NLP) algorithms are used for a variety of purposes. Basically, they help developers to make a software which understands human language and due to its complications, natural language processing is difficult to implement and learn correctly. With the passage of time, data scientists and machine learning engineers are working to improve this process and bring a better turnover rate.

Natural language processing algorithms are used to summarize blocks of text. To complete this operation, a summarizer is implemented into the machine learning model that extracts useful ideas and ignores any irrelevant information. Furthermore, the natural language processing models accurately generate keyword tags from the content through AutoTag which is an essential technique to discover the topics which are briefed in the content. Furthermore, the approach of sentiment analysis identifies the sentiment of a string from the given text in a positive manner.

The current approaches of natural language processing are dependent on deep learning concepts. Deep learning is a type of artificial intelligence that examines and utilizes patterns in data to improve the understanding abilities of a program. Earlier, the models of natural language processing were based on the rule-based approach which only had the capability to search for a phrase in the text and generate simple responses. Today, artificial intelligence and machine learning have greatly customized how natural languages processing models work and deliver outstanding results. Tools for NLP models are Gensim, Intel NLP Architect, and NLTK.

Python programming language comes with built-in libraries that help developers to create high end machine learning and artificial intelligence models. These libraries include SciPy, NumPy, and Pandas. Research is being done by data scientists to improve search results so that users can query datasets through a question and get accurate translation results in real-time. Machine learning models have the capability to understand vital elements of the human language and their sentence structure.

Key Advantages

Natural language processing models provide unlimited advantages. The model has the capability to improve efficiency and accuracy of documentation along with the opportunity to create a readable text summary. Moreover, this approach is the main driving force behind personal assistants like Alexa and Siri through which users can perform multiple tasks with ease.

Natural language processing provides long term benefits to companies as they can communicate with their clients effectively and solve queries in real-time through chatbots.

Data Handling in NLPs

The natural language processing systems are designed to understand conversations of different styles and languages. Data which is generated from declarations or conversations are a part of unstructured data. As compared to structured data, machine learning models find it difficult to comprehend unstructured data because there are no predefined relationships and labels. Natural language processing is a field of artificial intelligence that enables automated machines to learn, understand, and derive accurate meaning from human languages. This is only possible if the models are trained with labeled data so that they can easily comprehend multiple languages with a high accuracy rate.

Applications

Talent Recruitment

Human resource departments in various companies use natural language processing models to review resumes and conduct candidate interviews. In the search and selection process of talent recruitment, interviewers are able to identify the skills and abilities of potential hires and also review the latest trends in the job market.

Voice Assistants

Natural language processing tools such as Siri and Alexa work with AI models to respond from vocal prompts. Particularly, NLP models can do anything from finding a specific shop to scheduling an appointment for a given date. Voice assistants learn through structured data and need a lot of training data to develop an understanding of each language.

Health Care

Healthcare and medical departments have had great breakthroughs thanks to artificial intelligence and machine learning technologies. With the help of natural language processing tools, doctors and health specialists can explore more health conditions.

Impact of AI in Real Life

When searching about artificial intelligence and machine learning, we can find thousands of applications which are based on these technologies. Along with prediction and automation benefits, AI models can learn from huge amounts of data and allow people to collaborate with smart software. Nowadays, security cameras can search and identify people in real-time and track movements which is all possible through artificial intelligence.

Take for example hospitals and health care centers. Patients and doctors can get support from AI tools by calculating the prescribed level of activity or managing the recovery process. As a result, patients can recover quickly and maintain their health in a better way. Artificial intelligence technology is also implemented in online maps such as Google or Apple maps. The model has the capability to find the shortest route with the least amount of traffic so that travelers can reach their destination as quickly as possible.

In less than a decade, machine learning and artificial intelligence has greatly transformed into the mainstream of society and business. Although it is an impressive achievement, the cost of research and working on the technology is quite high. Take for example self-driving cars. We can see that such vehicles have the capability to control and manage speed without any kind of human intervention. To make this happen, the artificial intelligence technology in autonomous vehicles undergoes extensive training for which huge training datasets are required.

Self-driving vehicles work collaboratively as a connected network. This helps in predicting the behavior of pedestrians and other cars on the road in various scenarios.

Here are some essential applications of artificial intelligence designed through the Internet of Things (IoT):

Drones

Drones are small- and large-scale aircrafts which have the capability to fly and operate without human involvement. The piloting activities are controlled through a software and drones can navigate to unknown surroundings on their own. Drones are used for multiple purposes including surveillance, monitoring, security, and videography.

Retailing

Artificial intelligence is considered by retailers to observe customer behavior and requirements. There are several factors that need to be focused on when designing online shopping websites so that companies can avail a high number of sales in a short period of time. Moreover, sellers can also send personalized offers and discounts through AI models in their online stores.

Furthermore, artificial intelligence is best suited for gathering information about customer buying habits and preferences. This way, companies can bring significant improvements in sales and make more revenue in a short period of time. Online stores can also give recommendations to customers. This activity is done with the help of AI models as they analyze customer behavior and make suitable suggestions in real-time.

Email Filters

Email filters are based on artificial intelligence technology. Google has implemented email filters in Gmail which sort each email according to a predefined category. These categories include primary, social, promotions, updates, forums, and spam. Gmail sorts the received emails into five different categories and sends the spam messages to a separate folder. This is possible due to the implementation of artificial intelligence and machine learning models. Furthermore, Gmail also has a smart reply feature which automatically replies and respond to emails with simple words like "Thanks" just with a click of a button.

Sales and Marketing

Every large-scale industry and small-scale business are dependent upon the rate of sale and services to generate more profits. Data is divided into four major portions which includes volume, variety, velocity, and value. Artificial intelligence models validate purchase decisions and market trends of customers through these methods and allow companies to boost sales in a short period of time. With the evolvement of digital marketing, businesses can develop a strong online market presence without spending a fortune.

Predictive sales tools work similar to the conventional customer relationship management or CRM platforms because they can track and analyze thousands of events in real-time. Artificial intelligence programs have the power to scan through millions of events to determine correlations and patterns. Companies can only grow faster if they have selected the best suited machine learning and artificial intelligence model for their needs. Predictive sales are designed for companies to take advantage of the innovative ways in order to enhance their business.

Let's take Amazon as an example. It is a renowned online store and is integrated with state-of-the-art artificial intelligence algorithms. With the approach of evaluating shopping trends, AI models predict customer behavior and learn from purchase decisions as well. These types of algorithms have the capability to improve the decision-making process for companies.

Price Optimization and Forecasting

In real life, purchase decisions from people is highly dependent upon factors like discounts and promotions. Artificial intelligence algorithms can guide customers to the best suited purchase options and available discounts in real-time. Usually, sales managers have to overcome the challenges associated with the selling of products both physically and online. With the help of an AI algorithm, managers can forecast with a high degree of accuracy in order to increase sales and revenue for the company.

Employees who are responsible for lead scoring have to make decisions on a daily basis. There are many factors which need to be focused on before taking any steps so that no problems occur in the future. Most often, the decision-making process is dependent upon incomplete information and managers can tackle any kind of problem with the help of AI models. With the help of machine learning and artificial intelligence models, lead scoring managers can collect historical information for the respective client and study customer interaction history as well.

AI and Manufacturing

With every invention, manufacturing processes have completely transformed and received significant improvements in order to increase the quality and quantity from the production line. Nowadays, we can see that most manufacturers rely fully on robotics to accomplish significant components of their production line. New technologies which are based on artificial intelligence and machine learning models have the power to handle and automate routine activities in the production cycle with a high accuracy level. There is absolutely no doubt that artificial intelligence has now become the main driving force behind the manufacturing process of every industry.

Smart Maintenance

Each year, the manufacturing industry has to spend a huge amount of money on the maintenance and upgrade of the machines and systems. Although some parts need to be replaced and handled manually, most information systems and computer programs that control the whole process can be managed through artificial intelligence models. Predictive maintenance is an essential requirement for every manufacturing industry because it helps production line managers and auditors to overview turnover rates of the manufacturing cycle.

In artificial intelligence systems, predictive maintenance is done through advanced algorithms and artificial neural networks. By following this approach, companies can reduce downtime, costs, and effort required to upgrade systems. In cases where maintenance is needed regularly, technicians can be briefed beforehand about the specific components which need inspection.

Advantages of Using AI in Manufacturing

Smart manufacturing is the aim of every manufacturing industry. To make the process faster and more efficient, industries consider implementing high-end artificial intelligence and machine learning models in their information systems. Not only do AI models help in automating the process, but they also allow the whole manufacturing process to work smoothly and also learn while working for future improvements. With the help of automatic detection features, quality and assurance managers can figure out the loopholes and improve the overall quality of products.

Automating testing processes also helps in reducing the number of defects in a production line. Defects bring both financial and time loss to manufacturing companies because they sometimes fail to deliver orders on time. AI-powered machines have the capability to learn from previous production cycles and also help line managers in getting complete control over the work process. Moreover, the rate of human error in the production line is greatly reduced due to the implementation of automated robots.

On the other hand, production line managers can ensure optimized inventory control for the ongoing operations throughout the factory. Artificial intelligence and machine learning models also help in reducing the time spent on processes like machine calibration and fine tuning. All of these benefits could only be availed if the industries and manufacturing units are upgraded with the correct AI models.

Adapting Market Trends

Due to the ever-increasing competition and number of industries, manufactures have to study the market trends to make a strong recognition. Most of the time, companies end up with piled up stock in their inventories which is due to the lack of customer interest. Artificial intelligence algorithms play a vital role in optimization of manufacturing supply chains and allow companies to respond instantly to the market trends. This approach gives production line management the chance to work on effective strategies and meet the given deadlines without compromising on quality.

The manufacturing sector is best suited for the application and implementation of artificial intelligence. In the past, manufacturing lines were operated manually or with the help of traditional information systems. This often resulted in huge losses and manufacturers were unable to satisfy client requirements. Supply chain, production line, and administration problems can be easily identified and solved with the help of AI models.

Chapter 8: Deep Learning and Artificial Intelligence

Defining Deep Learning

The field of machine learning and artificial intelligence is dependent upon acquiring skills and learning experience through data. Machines can predict and automate processes without human intervention and deliver accurate data insights as well. Deep learning and machine learning are interrelated with artificial intelligence and work in collaboration to solve complex AI problems. To define the deep learning approach, we can consider it as a subset of machine learning. Furthermore, deep learning works similarly to the functionality of the human brain and allows AI models to predict and work in any situations like humans would.

The artificial neural network is designed on the basis of the human brain with multiple layers. There are three main layers including an input layer, an output layer, and a hidden layer. As compared to other categories of machine learning models, the deep learning systems need tons of data to be trained properly. In addition to training data, these algorithms need to be tested and evaluated regularly so that they do not lack in performance in any case.

Differences

The main difference between machine learning and deep learning is the ability to become progressive. Deep learning models need guidance and regular upgrades whereas the machine learning systems can analyze and upgrade on their own. The intent of artificial intelligence is to replicate a human brain and work in a similar procedure in order to boost performance, efficiency, and reliability. Apart from these major factors, deep learning models can make predictions for new scenarios with a high success rate.

Moreover, machine learning is different from expert systems and knowledge graphs because it can modify itself when trained with high quality training data. Machine learning models do not need human intervention to make changes in the system and work dynamically.

How Do Deep Neural Networks Work?

Deep neural networks are based on multiple layers and are a set of algorithms based on the architecture of the human brain. This approach is used to develop vital machine learning applications such as sound recognition, image recognition, natural language processing, and recommender systems. In a deep neural network, there are multiple hidden layers which allow the model to learn the features of training data. Moreover, the features are inherited from one layer to another to increase the prediction capabilities of the deep learning model. In a deep learning system, the information has to pass through multiple layers and is difficult to train as compared to other machine learning systems.

Similar to the machine learning models, deep learning systems have the capability to learn without being explicitly programed. This helps data scientists to achieve predictions of higher accuracy without the extra effort.

Deep Neural Networks in AI

A neural network is based on the concept of how the human brain actually works. Deep neural networks have a high level of complexity and they generally include more than two hidden layers. To make accurate decisions, deep neural networks use different kinds of mathematical modeling approaches to process data. Most experts consider deep neural networks as a way to simulate the performance of the human brain. Although it is not possible to achieve the same level of accuracy and decision-making abilities like humans do, deep neural network machines can differentiate between various scenarios and learn from both unstructured and structured data.

Applications

Below are a few applications of deep neural networks:

Voice Assistants

Voice activated assistants are one of the finest applications of deep neural networks. We already virtual assistants in our smartphones through which we can communicate and order the device to perform specific tasks. Natural language processing and machine learning techniques allow the voice assistance models to understand, interpret, and translate human voice into computer understandable format.

Automatic Machine Translation

Deep learning machines are best suited for developing real-time automatic machine translation tools. The automatic machine translation tools have the capability to translate the given text into another language in real-time. To complete this activity, the model need not need to be explicitly programed and can work perfectly even without any kind of human intervention. This model has the capability to perform automatic translation of text and images. The text translation can easily be performed without any kind of pre-processing on the sequence.

Image Recognition Tools

Image recognition tools are one of the finest inventions of deep learning. The model has the capability to identify objects and people in images by completing processing in real-time. Moreover, the image recognition approach is widely used in social media, tourism, retail, and gaming sectors. To activate image recognition, the model has to classify all of the objects in an image and detect the possible variables and attributes that will help in further identification.

Advertisement

In today's world, advertisement and marketing methods have completely transformed. The traditional means of advertisement have now been replaced with more trendy and attractive digital marketing tools. With the help of deep learning tools, we can perform data-driven predictive advertising and real-time bidding on ads. Furthermore, deep learning has made it easier for advertisers to leverage their content and get better insights in a short period of time.

Artificial Neural Networks

Similar to deep neural networks, artificial neural networks are also based on the architecture of the human brain. Most of the advancements made in the field of artificial intelligence such as robotics and voice recognition are done through artificial neural networks. Furthermore, artificial neural networks have the power to perform specific tasks such as clustering, classification, and pattern recognition. In addition to real-time processing, these networks can be configured to perform any task with ease.

A neural network is designed to get knowledge through the learning procedure. Moreover, the knowledge and data which is stored inside a neural network helps in making accurate decisions as well. The artificial neural networks can also be considered as weighted directed graphs. Neuron inputs and outputs are directly linked with one another which allows the network to communicate and retrieve information from external sources in the form of patterns and image vectors.

The perceptron model in neural networks has two input and one output units. The output units have no hidden layers and they are also known as single layer perceptron. In a multilayer perceptron neural network, we can have multiple hidden layers of neurons and this network is also known as feed forward neural network. Recurrent neural network is a type of network which has hidden neurons for developing self-connections. High performance neural networks are mandatory for performing practical operations.

Types of Learning

Similar to machine learning, there are different types of learning methods adopted by artificial neural networks. At first, the model is trained through the supervised learning approach in which the training dataset is provided to the network. After the training is complete, the desired outputs are named as weights which are then adjusted to achieve the desired outcomes. Unsupervised learning works directly opposite of the supervised learning approach because we already know the output that will be obtained through the given inputs. The network automatically classifies input data and sets the desired weight in the input data through the feature extraction process.

Reinforcement Learning

Reinforcement learning is a major part of machine learning and artificial intelligence. This approach is quite different from supervised learning. In the supervised learning training process, the model is given an answer key along with the training data but in the case of reinforcement learning, the model is supposed to decide what actions to take on the given task. This way, the model can learn and yield accurate results in the absence of a training dataset.

The main concepts in reinforcement learning are designed to deliver the best solution with the greatest reward. To operate the model, the input should be considered as an initial state from where the model will start its operation and several outputs can be expected because there are multiple solutions for a single problem. In machine learning models, the system only makes decisions as per the training dataset but with the reinforcement learning approach, we can easily solve unknown problems as well.

During the training process, the model will return to a specific state and allow the user to punish or reward the model based on the given output. After providing the best suited output, the model keeps on learning and improves over time. Reinforcement learning is widely used in AI application and model development.

Types

The two types of reinforcement learning are positive reinforcement learning and negative reinforcement learning. In positive reinforcement learning, an event is known to occur as a result of a particular behavior which in return increases the frequency and strength of the behavior. Positive reinforcement learning maximizes performance and gives increased lifespan to the reinforcement learning model.

On the other hand, negative reinforcement learning is an approach used to strengthen behavior of the reinforcement model to avoid a negative condition. In this way, reinforcement learning is able to increase behavior and deliver accurate defiance to a minimum standard of performance.

Uses and Implementation

Reinforcement learning is used in variety of deep learning model development processes. Mostly, the approach is considered to be used for data processing and machine learning model development. Apart from this, we can use reinforcement learning for industrial automation, robotics, and development of training systems. The reinforcement learning model development approach can also be used in large environments where the model of the environment is known but there is no analytical solution available.

This category of deep learning can only be used in large environments and is the only possible solution to collect information for interaction purposes. Reinforcement learning algorithms have the power to solve complex problems by delivering an immediate response. Because they have the minimum learning time, the model performs faster than any other approach in artificial intelligence and machine learning. Furthermore, it can also operate efficiently in a delayed return environment where it often becomes difficult to understand what action can lead to which outcome.

In real life environments, reinforcement algorithms perform better as they have the capability to select from an arbitrary number of actions instead of limited options. Through this, we can expect companies and businesses to achieve better outcomes and reduce the effort required to achieve desired goals.

Reinforcement Learning and Neural Networks

Neural networks are the best available function approximators and are particularly used in the development of reinforcement learning. Even when the action or state space is too large, the model can execute by using the available information and yield accurate insights in real-time. Furthermore, neural networks are also considered to calculate a value function through which it can learn to map state actions and values in the model. Each neural network makes use of coefficients to work on the functions and to relate inputs to outputs. The learning approach works to figure out the right coefficients and weights by making adjustments iteratively.

In the reinforcement learning model, we can also use convolutional networks to recognize states of the agents whereas the convolutional networks work in an opposite direction because they are designed to interpret from images in reinforcement learning. Apart from this, convolutional networks are great performers and deliver accurate results in any given scenario.

Is Deep Learning Better Than Machine Learning?

Although machine learning, artificial intelligence, and deep learning are amazing concepts, there are slight differences in each of the technologies which make them unique from one another. Deep learning and machine learning have a unique problem-solving approach because deep learning is designed to solve the problem in one part. To derive a solution for any scenario through machine learning technology, data scientists are required to break up the problem into different parts and derive separate use cases for each portion. Furthermore, a deep learning algorithm might take more time to train as compared to the machine learning model which takes only a few hours to train.

Another major difference between the two technologies is the power of interpretability. For example, if we are required to calculate the relevance score for a given document, deep learning algorithms are not best suited for this because it is unable to identify how the score is achieved. In the case of the machine learning model, powerful algorithms such as logistic regression and decision trees make it convenient to derive perfect solutions without effort. Although both deep learning and machine learning approaches have their own benefits, we need to first research and select the model which is best suited to solve the given problem.

In cases where there is less domain knowledge given for feature introspection, we can consider the approach of deep learning because it is designed to have a high-end infrastructure that trains in real-time. When it comes to solving complex problems like natural language processing, speech recognition, and image classification, deep learning technology is definitely the best option to be considered.

Impact of Deep Learning on Businesses

Most of the deep learning applications developed until now are able to reduce operational costs and enhance efficiency in businesses of all kinds. To implement this major change in the information system of any company, data scientists and deep learning engineers are required to perform in-depth research and evaluation so that the company is able to achieve long term benefits. Image recognition, speech and text analysis, risk assessment, content curation, and predictive maintenance are few of the major applications of artificial intelligence which have brought about great benefits for the corporate sector.

The applications mentioned above follow incremental approaches of working and bringing great improvements to the existing business models. In this way, companies can reduce operational costs and increase revenue within a short period of time. Most of the time, data scientists and machine learning engineers thoroughly study the work procedure and operations of any business before recommending a deep learning application. In the future, we can surely expect deep learning to become a major part of the software development process.

Risk Mitigation and Challenges

Generally, artificial intelligence and deep learning models have to face a wide range of risks and challenges for a business. Most of the time, confused managers and business leaders find it difficult to evaluate deep learning and are unable to understand its mathematical properties. In return, they are not able to achieve maximum efficiency and high-performance rates from the deep learning or machine learning model. Remember that deep learning is only suitable for mining unstructured datasets and companies should select a model after extensive research so that they do not end up purchasing oversold products.

The vast majority of companies and business are unaware about vital data science resources. Ethical issues and new liabilities are big challenges that are faced during the deployment of deep learning models in a business. Inadvertent discrimination and encoded judgement are the main problems deep learning models have to undergo. Furthermore, deep learning is directly improving the capabilities of artificial intelligence models and how they work to accomplish various projects. Just like the human brain functions, deep learning networks form associations between nodes in the data which can be directly controlled through the given software.

Business Automation

The process of business automation is done through artificial intelligence, machine learning, and deep learning technologies. Although there are several other methods to automate business processes and reduce the need for human workforce, managers are required to select the deep learning model after extensive research so that it can deliver long term benefits. Moreover, we can also reduce the main causes of human errors in daily business operations by guiding the employees on how to use and operate the models effectively.

Cost Reduction

When automating workflows, companies and businesses end up spending huge amounts of money. This usually happens when a company is unable to analyze their process requirements and select a large-scale AI model. Although machine learning and deep learning models are designed to deliver accurate results and prediction in every scenario, it is compulsory that you select the product which is exclusively designed for your business and does not have any kind of loopholes. To get help in this regard, users must also study the requirements and limitations of the AI software being used.

Chapter 9: The Fourth Industrial Revolution with AI

The fourth industrial revolution is an approach to define the differences between digital, biological, and physical worlds. Due to ever-increasing development and research, the information technology sector is receiving significant improvements with time. These advancements are conducted through the concepts of artificial intelligence, machine learning, the Internet of Things, genetic engineering, and any other major technology. The fourth industrial revolution consists of the technology that we are using today and which has brought significant improvements in the way we work and accomplish different tasks.

The third industrial revolution was also known as the digital revolution which also brought great advantages for businesses. The fourth industrial revolution is set to change information systems and workflows in new ways to allow increased production rates and effectiveness of businesses. People who are new to business need to understand how technologies work and what are the best suited information systems for their company.

Major Changes in Technology

The fourth industrial revolution brought about great changes and outcomes for businesses. With the help of artificial intelligence, business owners are able to track changes and solve complex problems without any hassle. Furthermore, artificial intelligence also helps in drawing conclusions, processing information, and recognizing complex patterns without human intervention. In this way, companies can conduct secure business operations and benefit from predictions without any hassle.

Take for example block chain technology. This approach is a decentralized and secure way of sharing and recording data. Companies now do not need to rely on third party intermediaries to accomplish routine tasks in their business. Not only will this reduce the overall operational costs, but also reduce the stress and involvement of employees required to complete the process. Bitcoin is a popular digital currency and is considered as the best blockchain application ever developed.

Furthermore, the fourth revolution in artificial intelligence has brought about new computing technologies that are making information systems smarter and more effective over time. Now, computers are able to obtain data and information from external resources such as the cloud and databases to process in real-time. This approach is absolutely dependent upon artificial intelligence and deep learning concepts of data handling and model training. Let's look at quantum computing as an example. We can see that computers have become thousands of times more powerful and efficient as compared to the traditional computing systems. Not only has this revolution benefited businesses greatly, but humans have also been granted ease and comfort through the implementation of AI in everyday activities.

Business Processes and Research

Design, manufacturing, and production industries have significantly improved due to the implementation of artificial intelligence and machine learning models. Take for example automated robots. We will soon be seeing robot assistants in homes, restaurants, and offices. Currently, robots are used for both commercial and personal use for health, safety, and human assistance purposes. The Internet of things is also an essential part of the automation and design process for machine learning and artificial intelligence models. There are several industrial applications including the addition of IoT sensors in farms, factories, and restaurants to get information related to product development and maintenance.

Impacts on the Future

The fourth industrial revolution is bringing about great advantages and immense support in today's world. Here are a few of the major impacts the upcoming technologies will bring which will completely transform the workflow and management in different fields.

Remote Work

The trend of hiring candidates remotely is increasing with each day. This approach was considered because sometimes companies are unable to find the best suited candidate for the job posting and have to employ specialist contractors. With the latest advancement in technology, we can see a huge increase in the rate of remote hiring. Not only is this approach beneficial for companies, but employees also enjoy the freedom of working and delivering better output. Moreover, employers are now become more supportive and open to allowing their existing employees to work remotely and complete the assigned tasks within the given deadline from a remote location.

Safe Working Environments

The implementation of new technologies has made it convenient for employees to work without any kind of safety concerns. With the implementation of a deep learning algorithm, security cameras are able to detect human behavior and take immediate action if any kind of fraudulent activity is detected. Moreover, if a dangerous situation has occurred, the applied system will automatically generate alerts to the concerted safety officer.

Future of Work

The biggest advancements and impacts ever given to the corporate sector are from artificial intelligence and machine learning models. Every day, thousands of manual processes are automated and with the advancements in technology, the activities will only continue to develop within the next few years. For global industries like finance, logistics, and aerospace, the Internet of things is the best suited approach to automate routine activities. To make this happen, companies will have to understand the need for artificial intelligence and machine learning models.

Increasing global competitiveness also results in more cost pressure. Eventually, this will result in substantial downsizing of employees. We need to understand that economic growth is dependent upon four factors of production. These factors include enterprise, capital, labor, and land. Today, the entrepreneurial capacity is decreasing with each passing year because large and established companies take advantage of AI and machine learning technologies.

However, the world must always focus on encouraging small scale businesses and entrepreneurs as well. In this way, we can easily develop a strong and interconnected network of business which in return will bring long term benefits to the world economy.

Training and Education

Education is an essential part of life for every human. Due to the latest advancements in technologies, educational institutions have also received major upgrades recently. From e-books to online notes, students are given access to every required piece of information through the click of a button. This has also improved performance and learning capabilities of students as they are able to study and understand concepts in a better way. With the help of graphical representations, visuals, and tutorials, teachers and students can cover the syllabus in a more effective manner.

Aside from the educational sector, the fourth industrial revolution has also improved the way in which employees are trained in the corporate sector. Nowadays, employers are focusing on achieving their business objectives in a short period of time for which training of employees is mandatory. Moreover, the ever-changing tools and technologies have also resulted in the need for efficient training and skill development tutorials for employees.

Advantages of the Fourth Industrial Revolution

When talking about the major advantages and benefits of the fourth industrial revolution, we can see significant improvements thanks to artificial intelligence, machine learning, and deep learning technologies. From automated cars to enhanced business processes, we can now see artificial intelligence in every field. Despite the challenges we are facing in today's world, artificial intelligence and machine learning technologies have greatly helped people in learning new skills and abilities in a short period of time.

Furthermore, we can also see a sound collaboration between policy makers, academia, and private sector companies as they have started to work together to achieve better outcomes. We can bring positive changes in our world and make it easier for people to accomplish everyday tasks without added stress.

How Has the Education Sector Transformed?

Due to the significant changes received from the fourth industrial revolution, we can notice great improvements in the education sector. Lecturers and teachers have followed the best approaches to help students in covering the syllabus and improve the overall learning process as well. Apart from these advantages, we are still required to give essential training for humanity and ethics to the students so that they are able to use technology without bringing harm to anyone.

Furthermore, teachers can also improve the way they are delivering ideas and concepts to the students. Teaching can be easily personalized with the help of artificial intelligence and machine learning models for which only a slight training on how to use the AI models is necessary and will allow teachers to bring significant improvements in the overall process.

Advantages for Development

In today's world, there are several countries that lack basic technologies. To make things simple for people living in the underworld countries, we are required to spread awareness and guidance about the benefits of information technology. This a major issue and needs to be handled immediately so that everyone can improve their living standards. The macro and micro social and economic policies should also be considered when implementing information technology.

In addition to making life easier, machine learning and artificial intelligence models also help individuals in developing better skills and abilities so that they can easily compete in the fast-growing corporate environment.

Along with these advantages, we can also get additional support and help from technology. New technologies are expected to provide a major influence in the agriculture industry in order to improve the quality and quantity of production. Although there are several challenges that need to be solved, we can learn from our past experiences and select the technology which is easy to use and delivers the best possible outcomes.

Artificial intelligence, machine learning, and deep learning technologies are only able to deliver accurate insights and high-performance rates if they are trained by structured and labeled datasets. Because AI models are implemented in routine, data scientists and experts have to make sure that the system is reliable and yields positive results in each case. When searching for the best information system technology, businesses and companies will surely find no better match as compared to artificial intelligence and machine learning models.

How Is AI Changing Our Lifestyles?

Artificial intelligence has brought great improvements and positivity in our daily lives. With the introduction of these technologies, we can accomplish routine activities and manage everyday tasks without the extra burden. Although each technology comes with amazing benefits and support, there are also several negative impacts that AI has on our daily lives. Due to automation, the need for human workforce is decreasing by each day which is in turn affecting employees and workers who are working daily wages. Artificial intelligence is bringing new concepts for designing machines that are used for automation purposes as well.

Disadvantages of AI

Although the basic concept of developing machine learning and artificial intelligence technologies is to make human life simpler, there are many negative aspects that need to be handled. Here are some of the few drawbacks of using artificial intelligence technology:

Ethics

Machines are prone to sentiments and ethics. As they are completely unaware of human emotions, feelings, and relationships, they fail to differentiate between right and wrong because they are simply programed to complete a given task. Therefore, machine learning and artificial intelligence engineers find it difficult to program machines for understanding human cultures, norms, and traditions. Not only in regard to workplace ethics, intelligent machines cannot understand human requirements on their own until the message is fully conveyed. Moreover, machines are also absolutely unaware about the religious and social norms which might not be acceptable for everyone.

Unemployment

This is by far the greatest fear which has resulted due to the implementation of artificial intelligence and machine learning systems in the workforce. Due to the capital-intensive technologies, the need for human workforce is reducing with each passing day which is definitely an alarming situation. In the future, if human beings fail to add more skills to their resumes, they might lose their jobs earlier than expected because artificial intelligence and machine learning systems are continuously being updated. Nowadays, people do not have the desired skills and abilities to operate machine learning models in order to obtain the best results.

Increased Operational Cost with No Improvement

As we have discussed earlier, the cost of purchasing and implementing machine learning and artificial intelligence systems is a lot higher in comparison to traditional information systems. Apart from the cost factor, artificial intelligence models are unable to improve from experience and they can only perform the same function until a new command is given. Also, artificial intelligence systems require tons of training data in order to work efficiently which can result in future problems for small-scale businesses.

Moreover, artificial intelligence models have no sense of improvement and they will keep on learning on a predefined pattern. Most of the time, they also fail to differentiate between an inefficient and a hardworking employee. The pros and cons of artificial intelligence technology need to be evaluated so that the approach does not bring harm to the human lifestyle in any case. Furthermore, we as humans need to understand the impacts of technology and bring improvements in our living standards in a convenient way.

Dangers Associated with AI Technology

Although artificial intelligence and machine learning technologies offer amazing benefits and support in our everyday lives, we also need to understand that artificial intelligence can be dangerous if not implemented in the correct manner. Taking autonomous weapons as an example, the product is allowed to make decisions on its own and in the case that it is misused, the results will be absolutely horrific. Furthermore, autonomous weapons are surely programed to kill and people need to be careful when handling such products to avoid any kind of loss to mankind.

Social media involvement is increasing by each day and most social media platforms are powered by artificial intelligence and machine learning algorithms. Facebook, for example, is the world's most powerful social media platform. It has the permission to access any user's information and could result in future security problems. Recently, data manipulation acts were reported for social media platforms through which personal data of millions of users was compromised. This is definitely a main drawback of artificial intelligence and it can target users in different ways.

Privacy concerns is yet another major issue that has resulted due to the implementation of artificial intelligence. The life and activities of an individual can easily be tracked from online platforms for which artificial intelligence models are completely responsible. Furthermore, security agencies can easily track and identify the movement of people through AI powered cameras. In the near future, the cost of implementing artificial intelligence models will increase and this is a major concern for companies and businesses who are working to automate their work processes. Furthermore, replicating human intelligence can also result in ethical concerns for a specific group as machines have started to work in similar ways to human beings.

AI as a Career

To begin a long-term career in artificial intelligence, individuals are required to have a specific educational background and skill set. Learning the high-level concepts of math, statistics, probability, calculus, algorithms, and algebra is mandatory to begin with the study of artificial intelligence. For model development and design, you have to learn graphical modeling, engineering, and robotics concepts in computer science.

Students who have strong concepts of high-level programming languages like Python and Java can start their career in artificial intelligence with ease.

The fourth industrial revolution has brought fundamental changes in the way we work, live, and relate to one another. The process of human development has made significant improvements in ways that are all possible with the addition of extraordinary technological advances. Furthermore, these advances are connecting digital, biological, and physical worlds in a way that creates great potential for humans in the upcoming years.

Chapter 10: Future of AI

There is surely no competitor to artificial intelligence technology as the approach has truly transformed multiple operations all over the world. In the past few years, researchers and data scientists have worked hard to invent intelligent machines and business models that can bring long term advantages. Furthermore, the process of data handling, collection, and manipulation has helped all major industries including education, healthcare, finance, and information technology to accomplish complex tasks without any inconvenience.

It is mandatory to understand the goal of artificial intelligence and how it will transform our world in the upcoming years. According to machine learning and artificial intelligence engineers, the technology is in its initial stage of growth and has to receive major breakthroughs with the passage of time. Furthermore, intelligent machines will also be given the power to differentiate between right and wrong, similar to human intellect. The final goal of AI is to develop a machine which is capable of meeting the level of human intellect.

How Will AI Change Our Lives?

The speed of development for artificial intelligence technology is fast and we need to speedily adapt to this new form of technology to make our lives convenient. Every day, we are noticing continued development and upgrades in new technologies and applications which is also tough competition for developers and computer scientists. There are four main reasons why artificial intelligence will change our lives forever. The first is that it will affect the way we work, the way we handle everyday situations, and the way we are living. Furthermore, with the progress of this technology, we will have to make adjustments in our lives so that the information systems are adapted in a suitable manner.

The widespread use of automation and robotics will somehow reduce the need for human workforce. AI is working to completely automate manufacturing units so that companies can finish more tasks in a certain period of time with better performance and accuracy. Furthermore, repetitive tasks can easily be done with the support of AI robots and intelligent machines instead of hiring workforce which is costly and less time efficient. Artificial intelligence is empowering the process for autonomous operations of all kinds. Take for example autonomous vehicles. We can see that the need for human drivers isn't needed as self-driving vehicles can study the immediate surroundings and operate without human intervention. While on the road, the machine learning model implemented in self-driving vehicles learns for future developments as well.

In addition to the automation of our work lives, artificial intelligence is expected to become a major part of overall human activities. We can use AI systems to interact with each other, increase our creativity, and get predictions for future plans without any hassle. Take the example of writing aid tools. AI models immediately give guidance about sentence structure, phrases, and grammar once the writer has submitted the text for editing. Each of the operations is done in real-time so that writers can enhance their creativity and writing skills.

Enhanced Communications

Apart from automating tasks, AI models are quite social and can be trained to communicate with people for hours. As machines never get annoyed or irritated, unlike humans, they can translate different languages in order to understand the communication in real-time. Moreover, machine learning models are able to understand nuance, colloquialisms, and context to fill the gap in human communication.

Information Access

In the future, we will be given more access to hidden information. This activity is being conducted by machine learning models during their operational period as they have the power to find hidden labels, attributions, and information in the collected datasets. Even after years of research and evaluation, humans might not be able to fetch information in a way that the intelligent machines can. As humans, we often don't have the patience to give out information to others or for any other activity. This task can be effectively done with the help of artificial intelligence models as they are widely used in human resource departments all over the world. Moreover, the future of AI will deliver outstanding benefits to companies and businesses as they can read information through predictions and calculations which can bring long term advantages.

Upcoming Big Data Trends

The accessibility of data has received major breakthroughs and upgrades within the development of big data models. Big data analytics have now become an essential part of the information gathering process in business intelligence and most businesses are getting long term benefits out of it as well. New concepts and methodologies of big data are constantly being launched to replace older technologies. With the help of intelligent business systems and artificial intelligence models, the financial sector can handle millions of transactions with high level security and efficiency.

Different approaches and methods from the Internet of things are also being developed to achieve better streaming analytics and performance of data handling models. Typically, data present in data storage centers is stored for training in a controlled environment. With the support of useful information, machine learning models can make predictions in real-time by reviewing the labels, relationships, and attributes from the training data. Remember that the aim of working for the improvement of big data processes is to give more appropriate responses and solutions to companies in each scenario.

AI Platforms

Artificial intelligence platforms continue to deliver long-lasting support and opportunities to machine learning and data science engineers for developing new models. By using artificial intelligence platforms to handle big data, companies and businesses can improve efficiency and achieve sales targets within a short period of time. Furthermore, AI platforms also support efficient communications with staff and data scientists so that management of the respective company can get complete details regarding every process.

There are different layers of AI platforms which give users the access and permission to perform certain operations on the data. The layers of AI platforms are mentioned as follows:

- Data and integration layer
- Experimentation layer
- Operations and deployment layer
- Intelligence layer
- Experience layer

Starting with the data and integration layer, users can get access to data and there is no need to give further instructions to the AI model for data handling purposes. Next is the experimentation layer from where the data scientists can develop, test, and run any kind of hypothesis. In the operations and deployment layer, there is a predefined governance model and deployment facilities are given so that users can utilize the available components for using the AI platform.

The intelligence layer in AI platforms organizes and provides intelligent services to support the artificial intelligence model. At last, the experience layer is made to interact with users in real-time as it is based on the technologies like gesture control augmented reality and conversational user interface. To enhance the performance and reliability of artificial intelligence platforms, data scientists get help from data curators as well. The role of a data curator is to manage the organizations metadata, data quality, and data governance features.

Moreover, data curators also work to provide presentations showing the performance of the artificial intelligence platform. Not only this, data curators also help in learning about the efficiency and reliability of traditional information systems as well. To handle data remotely, the trend of using hybrid cloud storage centers is increasing. Whenever an organization has to save data, it can work through the tools and features of the hybrid system.

Smart Machines

To meet the increasing demand for smart machines, manufacturers are adding intelligent information systems in electronic devices to bring ease to their customers. Taking the example of a smart home, we can take note of features such as automatic home protection, light control systems, and comfort management features. Each of the features are accessible at smart phones through which people can make relevant adjustments even if they are away from their home. These features are purely based on sensors and artificial intelligence models because they can learn and adapt the living habits of residents as well.

Features of smart homes include safety, security, energy and cost management, comfort, and entertainment. Without the need to program the system regularly, people can also communicate with AI bots to give certain orders. Once the order has been received in the system, it is automatically translated into a machine-understandable format through natural language processing tools. Moreover, the smart home system also has a function to detect unwanted activities such as theft and report the concerned authorities in real-time. Smart homes function to deliver unmatchable comfort and peace of mind with the help of automation features.

Personal assistants like Alexa or Siri are expected to be implemented in smart homes as well. With the development of artificial intelligence technology, people will get outstanding benefits and ease in performing routine tasks.

Upcoming AI Technologies

Meta learning is an expected AI technology which will help machines in studying information and make better predictions than before. Until now, machine learning and deep learning models have the capability to work only in the environment for which they are designed. To enhance the working capacity of machines, data scientists are working to explore the broad spectrum of artificial intelligence and solve the limitations in AI models as well. With the introduction of generative models, it will surely become easier to incorporate AI solutions into complex information systems.

For the rational and intuitive machines, the concepts of artificial intelligence will be revised in order to find new relationships in data and learning models. The concept of artificial intelligence is known to receive major upgrades and improvements in the upcoming years which will in turn bring long term benefits for businesses and industries.

Deep Learning Environments

To get better results and outcomes from a deep learning model, it is mandatory that the system is working in a controlled environment. A hybrid solution can be derived to create an AI environment which is directly trained by human beings so that AI models make predictions similar to humans. Deep learning training process is one of the most difficult parts of the artificial intelligence ecosystem. In fact, it also involves the handling of neural systems and machine learning concepts to deliver accurate insights and prediction results. On the other hand, future AI machines will be made capable of learning through interaction because it often becomes impossible to feed the artificial intelligence systems with training datasets.

Soon, we will be noticing new infrastructures and development environments which are focused on the approaches of deep learning. It will become easier for machines to interact and experiment in a specific environment. With the support of conversational cognition, we can understand the objective of high-profile developments and systems in artificial intelligence. In the future, developments in artificial intelligence will be based on the application of intuitive intelligence and meta learning.

Artificial General Intelligence

Artificial general intelligence are actually intelligence systems which have the ability to make decisions and think generally without depending upon previous training. Unlike simple artificial intelligence and machine learning models, artificial general intelligence systems are highly complex and have the power to make accurate decisions based on their own findings. For these reasons, artificial intelligence models remain limited and sometimes it becomes impossible for them to make accurate predictions and data insights.

Researchers are working to make artificial general intelligence (AGI) technology safer for humans. AGI systems have no room for error and they are programed to accomplish the given task no matter what the circumstances are. This approach is often considered as a safety concern for humans because AGM models will never divert from their path, even if people are getting affected. Take for example automated machine guns. If they are programed with the AGM model, they will certainly complete the expected round of fire and finish at the given target without analyzing the impacts this has on others. To make things safer and more peaceful for humans, artificial general intelligence is not widely implemented because research and evaluation is being done to make this approach safe and reliable.

Artificial Narrow Intelligence

The artificial narrow intelligence approach is defined as an AI model's ability to perform a specific task with one-hundred percent accuracy. Although artificial intelligence and machine learning models can perform multiple tasks at a time, in the case of artificial narrow intelligence, the computer program is only supposed to perform a single task without any errors or mistakes. Typically, the artificial narrow intelligence model is implemented in robots because they have to perform a single task several times. Due to its strong understanding and learning capabilities, artificial narrow intelligence allows intelligent machines to deliver the best outcomes in each transaction.

Artificial Super Intelligence

The concept of artificial super intelligence is referred to as the ability for computers to surpass human imagination and thoughts. As a result, super computers will become superior to humans and might perform activities that result in serious problems. Data scientists and researchers are working to develop a computer which can simulate the cognitive ability and knowledge similar to that of an adult human. Although several experiments are being performed, there is still no computer developed which can replace the thinking and analytical performance of a human.

However, there is still the chance of introducing artificial super intelligence for the benefit of human beings. Processes and tasks which cannot be automated with the help of conventional artificial intelligence systems can be easily done by implementing artificial super intelligence models.

Chapter 11: Essentials, Computer Vision, and AI

Machine learning is a modern-day approach which has always helped businesses in achieving long term goals. Although it is a subset of artificial intelligence, it is being regularly used to manufacture high performance automated learning systems. The concepts and findings of machine learning models are similar to the artificial intelligence models because both work in a similar manner. With the availability of concurrent methods and approaches, data scientists and machine learning engineers can perform complex tasks such as prediction, learning, regression, and classification.

Regression and Classification

Regression and classification in machine learning algorithms are considered as the best practice to discover patterns from big data. With the passage of time, data scientists make use of different techniques in artificial intelligence and machine learning. In supervised machine learning model, regression is used where we are given input variable (x) along with an output variable (y). Regression algorithm is used to learn the map function through inputs and outputs. Furthermore, the aim of using the regression model in machine learning is to predict accurate outputs for variable (Y) as well.

In case of classification, we can see that the model attempts to draw conclusions from observed values. Classification can be easily done with the help of supervised learning in artificial intelligence and machine learning.

Web Mining

Web mining is a technique used for discovering and extracting information from web services and documents. This approach helps users to extract meaningful information from websites present over the Internet. This information is also used to feed machine learning and artificial intelligence models. Web mining is also suitable to predict user behavior and how people are responding in certain scenarios.

The technique of web mining is divided into three main categories which are web content mining, web usage mining, and web structure mining. In web content mining, the application is responsible for extracting useful and required information from the Internet which is then used for different purposes. This approach of mining is also known as text mining because it performs complete scanning and evaluation of images, texts, and various web pages.

For the web usage mining approach, the application is responsible for discovering interesting facts and patterns from large datasets. Large datasets can be extracted with the help of machine learning methods. After the extraction procedure is complete, the next stage is to find user access data present on the web and collect the vital information in the form of logs.

Web structure mining is the process of discovering patterns and structure information from the Internet. The structure and information that is available on the website also has a relationship with other commercial websites which often makes it difficult for developers to extract the required information. Web structure mining is the most popular and unique web mining approach because of its simplicity and uniqueness.

Computer Vision

Computer vision is a field of study which helps computers to see and understand the context of digital images. Being a powerful and important type of artificial intelligence, researchers and data scientists are working to bring significant improvement in the development of computer vision models. This approach has the capability to replicate the complex parts within the human vision system and allow computers to perform different operations on images.

In the past, computer vision worked in a limited capacity and did not yield effective results but with the introduction of machine learning and artificial intelligence systems, researchers can work on bringing major upgrades and betterments in computer vision systems as well. The main driving force behind the growth of computer vision models is the volume of data which allows the algorithms to receive training and work effectively.

After the training procedure is complete, computer vision models are able to identify patterns and make suitable decisions without human intervention. Experiments for the development and upgrade of computer vision started in the early 1970s and have continued until now.

Working of Computer Vision Models

Machine learning and neural networks are based on the architecture of human brains. Each node in a human brain is interconnected and communicates with each other to make specific decisions in real-time. In the case of computer vision, the model is completely based on pattern recognition techniques that are used to detect variables and attributes as well. For example, if we give the computer vision model a million images of parrots, it will start learning about different characteristics like color, shapes, distances between each shape, and the type of border used in the image.

In this sense, computer vision models keep on learning and adapt to changes on their own. This work procedure is similar to machine learning and artificial intelligence models because they also tend to learn with training data and experience. Machines have the capability to interpret images by overviewing the properties like pixels, colors, and dimensions. To complete the image processing task, a lot of memory is required by the computer vision model because of iterations performed for each pixel in the image. Due to the huge amount of storage and computing power, this approach is quite different from other machine learning and artificial intelligence models.

Evolution and Design

Before the invention of deep learning networks, routine tasks and activities performed through computers were more prone to errors and mistakes. Today, developers can create state-of-the-art information systems and artificial intelligence models with the help of built-in libraries in major programming languages.

In order to perform facial recognition, we are required to create a database at first which includes all of the relevant images and information regarding the person. Each of the added files should be of the same format so that it does not get rejected by the computer vision model during processing. The next step is to annotate images for which you will be required to add several data points and information related to each file separately. After you are done with adding details, the next step is to give critical information related to the face structure of the person in the image.

To define a face structure, we can enter key data points like distance between the eyes, distance between the nose and upper lip and width of the jaw line. There are several other measurements which can be included to complete the information required for a computer vision model to operate effectively.

Annotations and Capturing Images

The process of annotation and capturing images is the main part of the computer vision model work procedure. You are required to capture clear images either from photographs or from video content so that the model can interpret the scenario without any hassle. After the process of capturing images is complete, next comes the task of annotation. Annotation activity is used to define properties of the required images.

Once each manual task is complete, the application is then able to process images and compare measurements in the new images as well. Remember that the new image is stored in the database where the computer vision model is located. There is quite a bit less automation involved as a whole since developers are required to complete most of the tasks manually.

How Are Convolutional Neural Networks and Computer Vision Interlinked?

Most of the advancements and progress achieved by the computer vision approach is because of convolutional neural networks. This model is a subset of deep learning and has to offer a few more operations which help in improving the accuracy and performance of computer vision models. Tasks related to image processing, management, and comparison can also be done with the help of convolutional neural networks.

Remember that convolutional neural networks are based on the concepts and findings of neural networks. For achieving a high level of accuracy and precision, the model works on external methods like feature extraction. This approach is ideal for handling images which have redundant information and are more informative as compared to the original provided input.

Applications

Here are some of the main applications of computer vision technology:

Autonomous Vehicles

Although self-driving or autonomous vehicles are based on machine learning and artificial intelligence models, computer vision technology also plays a vital role in the decision-making abilities of self-driving vehicles. By allowing cars to overview the surroundings, data scientists and machine learning engineers make use of cameras to capture accurate insights. This helps the car to observe its surroundings in real-time. Furthermore, self-driving vehicles can also learn with time by remembering driving trends of other cars.

Facial Recognition

Facial recognition tools are the finest implementation of computer vision technologies. With the help of facial recognition tools, security agencies and organizations can detect fraudulent activities and make preventive measures to avoid any loss in real-time. On the other hand, social media apps like Facebook have implemented facial recognition tools which help users to tag their friends through the given suggestions.

Healthcare

In health care and medical departments, computer vision technology is widely used. Computer vision algorithms in healthcare centers help researchers and doctors to automate vital tasks like observing x-ray reports and MRI scans to detect possible diseases. The healthcare and medical sector are one of the biggest users of artificial intelligence and computer vision models. With the implementation of these models, it has now become easier to detect problems by doctors and patients can ensure a speedy and effective recovery.

Augmented Reality

Augmented reality and mixed reality activities are performed with the support of a computer vision model. With the implementation of computer vision concepts, digital devices such as projectors, tablets, or smartphones are able to embed and overlay virtual objects through real world imagery. Furthermore, computer vision algorithms can also be used to display virtual objects without compromising on the overall quality of the image or video.

Challenges for Computer Vision Algorithms

Although computer vision algorithms are fine-tuned and have the power to perform multiple activities at a time, there are several important factors that lead to further challenges with the passage of time. Computer vision aids computers to see and observe in a way similar to human beings. The process is complex and there is a lot of research and observation required to develop a high-performing computer vision model.

Inventing machines similar to computer vision is a complex task for which artificial intelligence and machine learning engineers have to face a lot of difficulties.

Activities such as image segmentation and object detection are the biggest challenges faced by computer vision models. Image segmentation is the process to partition the given image through external properties and accurate boundaries. The process also covers the techniques of instance segmentation and semantic segmentation which are sometimes difficult to handle by the computer vision models.

Furthermore, the activity of object detection in a computer vision model often results in problems. To make things manageable, it is advised that only high-quality images and files are fed into the computer vision model so that it can complete the processing and workflow without any kind of interruption.

Humans Visual Understanding vs Computer Vision

There is surely no match for the observance and comprehending abilities of human eyes which makes humans a lot better at image understanding and evaluation. This happens because computer vision machines are narrow-sighted and do not have enough power to sense in the same way humans do. Although continuous learning and training allows computer vision models to comprehend images perfectly, there is still a lot of room left for improvement. Neocortex is the main driving force which enables humans to recognize patents and useful insights from any image or real-time observance.

There is absolutely no comparison of the human brain with artificially developed computer vision models. Although computer vision models are great performers, they certainly lack performance and processing abilities when compared with human eyes. Furthermore, humans are continuously collecting information and data at every point which is absolutely not the case with computer vision machines.

It is mandatory to train machine learning models until a predefined limit and in the case that they are fed with excessive data, there are chances that a malfunction might occur. In case of human eyes, constant usage of smartphones, computers, or continuous driving can result in pain or tears but the processing ability of a human eye is never affected in any case.

Future of Computer Vision

As we have already discussed how computer vision models work and process images, the field is expected to receive great improvements in the future. Computer vision is also considered as the ability of intelligent systems to see and perform specific functions similar to human beings. Although data scientists and machine learning engineers have developed high-performance computer vision models, there are still a lot of changes and improvements yet to be delivered.

However, the process of translating images is now becoming complex due to the increasing amount of high-definition images and videos. Computer vision models are required to handle, store, and manipulate the given images in order to perform multiple tasks such as facial recognition. With the ever-increasing requirements for machine learning and computer vision projects, data scientists and machine learning engineers have to consistently research and deliver more precise models.

State of Computer Vision

Computer vision technology is being consistently developed and is powered by state-of-the-art deep learning algorithms. The process also involves operations of convolutional neural networks which help in observing and making sense for the given images. Generally, neural networks are trained by using thousands of images which in return helps the algorithm to deliver accurate insights and remember image patterns as well. In context to the current situation of computer vision models, there is still a lot of room for improvements. Furthermore, computer vision is amazingly different from machine learning and deep learning models for which developers have to take care of different factors for improving their performance and reliability.

Although computer vision is different from other artificial intelligence models, it definitely delivers accurate results and has the power to analyze through different situations in real-time. Furthermore, computer vision is fully unprecedented and there is no other model of artificial intelligence which works in the same manner. Most people consider computer vision technology to work in similar ways to human beings but this is absolutely not the case. Artificial intelligence systems work similarly to human brains but can never substitute or replicate it in reality.

Image datasets which are fed by humans are sometimes not properly labeled and do not meet the criteria set by the computer vision models. In return, this directly affects the performance and prediction capabilities of the computer vision model. In machine learning, the models are programed to learn from experience and they also tend to improve over time. Similar is the case with computer vision models as they keep on learning during the prediction phase and use the gathered information to make improvements in the future.

Significance of AI Machines

We have thoroughly discussed and reviewed the main applications of artificial intelligence. Although most of them work in the same procedure, each model has a set of unique characteristics which make them different from each other. Although machine learning and artificial intelligence models have the capability to learn and develop on their own, they are still dependent upon humans to get started and improve over time.

With the introduction of artificial intelligence, data scientists have become successful in automating business, corporate, educational, healthcare, finance, and manufacturing processes. To avail best outcomes and high-end performance, it is mandatory that an artificial intelligence model is selected after proper research and evaluation. Furthermore, routine checks and upgrades of AI models also helps in getting better results.

Over the next few years, information systems and technologies are going to receive major breakthroughs. Because of the latest research and findings, artificial intelligence and machine learning models are able to develop and make a strong market presence.

The processes and tasks that are used in the development of machine learning and artificial intelligence models are also responsible for how the models perform in real life. Furthermore, the models are required to be long-lasting, supportive, and reliable so that they can be implemented in any industry with ease.

Last but not least, humans have received significant ease and benefits with the introduction of machine learning and artificial intelligence models. The way these models handle problems and calculate possible solutions has helped humans in achieving their work targets and goals in a short period of time. With traditional information systems, it often becomes difficult for people to perform the same activity in a routine manner and it also leads to a high rate of human error, but this problem is now completely solved with the development of machine learning and artificial intelligence algorithms.

We must remember the fact that artificial intelligence and machine learning models are developed by human beings and they might not yield accurate results in each transaction. To make things better, we can focus on routine training with high-quality data and tune the models to deliver accurate insights, predictions, and analyses. With the latest advancements and improvements, information technology will continue to bring long term benefits and advantages to humans.

Artificial Intelligence and Robots

Robots are developed with artificial intelligence and machine learning models because they have to perform multiple tasks without being explicitly programed. Most modern robots are capable of working in restaurants, hotels, and in production lines with the help of AI technology. Although robots do not have any generalized analytical ability, they can make predictions and find suitable actions to be performed. Furthermore, artificial intelligence robots continue to learn during the operation and navigation process. Most commonly, modern computers and information systems are used to design robots so that they can complete routine activities without any hassle. Some robots also have the capability to repeat human actions and learn the ways humans are performing specific actions.

Mostly, robots respond immediately to human commands because they are powered by natural language processing modules. With the implementation of natural language processing, robots can understand and interpret human language in real-time. Although it is a low-level interaction, machine learning experts and artificial intelligence engineers are working to create robots with amazing capabilities. On the other hand, the real challenge of making intelligent robots is to control them while they are operational. Once they have started to learn on their own, intelligent robots will work similar to humans and derive conclusions as well. However, robots are unaware about the importance of relationships and ethics which can result in future problems. Moreover, there are different ways to control how robots perform routine activities and we have to make sure they do not bring any harm to humans.

Features

Intelligent robots are programed to perform different tasks on their own. Most of them are based on six major patterns which includes lifting the left leg, releasing the left leg, lifting the right leg, releasing the right leg, lifting both legs together and releasing both legs together. Apart from these features, intelligent robots are able to speak and understand instructions as well. Robots are designed using the computer vision approach of artificial intelligence through which they can easily monitor and explore their surroundings.

Hardware for the computer vision system in a robot includes a power supply, camera, processor, software, display device for monitoring, and other accessories as well. Robotics are mainly used for handling material in the production line and other activities like polishing, drilling, color coating, and welding. Moreover, autonomous robots are widely used for military surveillance and security purposes. In the health care sector, intelligent robots are used to conduct routine clinical tests and also support in rehabilitating the permanently disabled. Furthermore, miniature robots are capable of performing surgeries as well.

It is mandatory to understand how artificial intelligence technologies work and make relevant predictions. Once you are aware about the concepts and findings of these technologies, developing intelligent systems and robots will surely not be a difficult task. The machine learning model is dependent upon training datasets through which they develop strong analytical and predictive skills. These techniques are developing continuously which, as a result, will bring great advantages to businesses and industries from all over the world.

Several research groups are being examined by the artificial intelligence department. Research subjects include natural language processing, robotics, computer vision, e-commerce, and computational biology. Over the next several years, intelligent robots and automated machines are expected to be used widely in homes, offices, and restaurants. Although a lot of training and exercise is needed to develop ideal robots, there are also several other key factors that need to be considered when developing artificial intelligence and machine learning robots.

Furthermore, the basic idea of artificial intelligence and computer science is to solve complicated problems and give suitable solutions which will benefit human beings. Although process automation and the widespread use of artificial intelligence has resulted in a few problems for human beings, the advantages outweigh the downfalls and are outstanding and benefit mankind. Artificial intelligence and machine learning models are developed to bring long term solutions and services for businesses and industries worldwide. Last but not least, the technology is currently in the development stage and is expected to bring major improvements in the future.

Conclusion

This book is an authentic and detailed guide about the amazing concepts, explanations, and benefits of artificial intelligence in our everyday lives. Artificial intelligence and machine learning models have revolutionized business processes and have brought about positive aspects for companies to improve their performance and achieve targets. With the help of AI models, data scientists are able to explore new horizons of technology and work to bring significant improvements and ease for human beings.

Starting from the history of artificial intelligence, this book has covered the concepts of artificial intelligence from a grass root level which makes it best suited for beginners. Moreover, graphical illustration of AI concepts along with detailed descriptions for each model makes it easier to learn and work with artificial intelligence technology. Furthermore, the business advantages, impacts, and significance of machine learning and artificial intelligence models will surely help beginners in adapting the given concepts. The need for AI system is increasing with each passing day for which data scientists and researchers are developing new techniques to get accurate predictions and data analytics from AI models. With the aim to deliver the concepts of artificial intelligence and its significance in a simple and clear manner, this book has been written exclusively for beginners so that they can learn the interesting concepts and theories of artificial intelligence.

References

Method and Goals in AI. Retrieved from https://www.britannica.com/technology/artificial-intelligence/Methods-and-goals-in-AI

Javaid. N, (Aug-2018) Machine Learning., retrieved from https://towardsdatascience.com/machine-learning-basics-part-1-a36d38c7916

Josh. (2015, December 28). Everything You Need to Know About Artificial Neural Networks. Retrieved from https://medium.com/technology-invention-and-more/everything-you-need-to-know-about-artificial-neural-networks-57fac18245a1

Margaret. R., Artificial Neural Network., retrieved from https://searchenterpriseai.techtarget.com/definition/neural-network

What is an Expert system?., retrieved from https://www.guru99.com/expert-systems-with-applications.html

Stuart. G., (2019). AI and its influence on HRM. Retrieved from https://www.onrec.com/news/news-archive/ai-and-its-influence-human-resource-management

A beginner's guide to important topics in AI. Retrieved from https://skymind.ai/wiki/deep-reinforcement-learning

Sambit. M.,(2019) Why deep learning over machine learning? Retrieved from https://towardsdatascience.com/why-deep-learning-is-needed-over-traditional-machine-learning-1b6a99177063

Michael. B., (2019) How can developing countries take advantage of the fourth industrial revolution? Retrieved from https://www.geospatialworld.net/blogs/how-can-developing-countries-take-advantage-of-the-fourth-industrial-revolution/

https://builtin.com/artificial-intelligence/artificial-intelligence-future

Ilijia. M., (2019) Everything you ever wanted to know about computer vision. Retrieved from https://towardsdatascience.com/everything-you-ever-wanted-to-know-about-computer-vision-heres-a-look-why-it-s-so-awesome-e8a58dfb641e